Brian Friel

THE IRISH WRITERS SERIES

James F. Carens, General Editor

TITLE	*AUTHOR*
SEAN O'CASEY	Bernard Benstock
J. C. MANGAN	James Kilroy
W. R. RODGERS	Darcy O'Brien
STANDISH O'GRADY	Phillip L. Marcus
PAUL VINCENT CARROLL	Paul A. Doyle
SEUMAS O'KELLY	George Brandon Saul
SHERIDAN LEFANU	Michael Begnal
AUSTIN CLARKE	John Jordan
BRIAN FRIEL	D. E. S. Maxwell
DANIEL CORKERY	George Brandon Saul
EIMAR O'DUFFY	Robert Hogan
MERVYN WALL	Robert Hogan
FRANK O'CONNOR	James Matthews
JAMES JOYCE	Fritz Senn
JOHN BUTLER YEATS	Douglas Archibald
LORD EDWARD DUNSANY	Zack Bowen
MARIA EDGEWORTH	James Newcomer
MARY LAVIN	Zack Bowen
OSCAR WILDE	Edward Partridge
SOMERVILLE AND ROSS	John Cronin
SUSAN L. MITCHELL	Richard M. Kain
J. M. SYNGE	Robin Skelton
KATHARINE TYNAN	Marilyn Gaddis Rose
LIAM O'FLAHERTY	James O'Brien
IRIS MURDOCH	Donna Gerstenberger
JAMES STEPHENS	Brigit Bramsback
BENEDICT KIELY	Daniel Casey
EDWARD MARTYN	Robert Christopher
DOUGLAS HYDE	Gareth Dunleavy
EDNA O'BRIEN	Grace Eckley
CHARLES LEVER	M. E. Elliott
BRIAN MOORE	Jeanne Flood
SAMUEL BECKETT	Clive Hart
ELIZABETH BOWEN	Edwin J. Kenney
JOHN MONTAGUE	Frank Kersnowski
ROBERT MATURIN	Robert E. Lougy
GEORGE FITZMAURICE	Arthur E. McGuinness

MICHAEL MCCLAVERTY
FRANCIS STUART
PATRICK KAVANAGH
BRINSLEY MACNAMARA
  AND GEORGE SHIELS
STEPHEN MACKENNA
JACK B. YEATS
WILLIAM ALLINGHAM
SAMUEL LOVER
FLANN O'BRIEN
DENIS JOHNSTON
WILLIAM LARMINIE
SIR SAMUEL FERGUSON
LADY GREGORY
GEORGE RUSSELL (AE)

DION BOUCICAULT
THOMAS DAVIS
LOUIS MACNEICE
PADRAIC COLUM

Leo F. McNamara
J. H. Natterstad
Darcy O'Brien
Raymond J. Porter

Roger Rosenblatt
Robin Skelton
Alan Warner
Mabel Worthington
Bernard Benstock
James F. Carens
Richard J. Finneran
Malcolm Brown
Hazard Adams
Richard M. Kain and
  James O'Brien
Peter A. Tasch
Eileen Ibarra
Christopher Armitage
Charles Burgess

BRIAN FRIEL

D. E. S. Maxwell

Lewisburg
BUCKNELL UNIVERSITY PRESS

#60151

© 1973 by Associated University Presses
Associated University Presses, Inc.
Cranbury, New Jersey 08512

Library of Congress Cataloging in Publication Data

Maxwell, Desmond Ernest Stewart, 1925–
    Brian Friel.

    (The Irish writers series)
    Bibliography: p.
    1. Friel, Brian.
PR6056.R5Z8   822'.9'14   76-125299
ISBN 0-8387-7753-8
ISBN 0-8387-7666-3 (pbk.)

Printed in the United States of America

Contents

Author's Note

I am deeply grateful to Brian Friel for being most liberal with his time and patience during my preparation of this study, though it should be understood that Mr. Friel's kindness confers no special authority on my remarks.

I am indebted as well to John Boyd and Ronald Mason of the British Broadcasting Corporation, both for their assistance in directing me to radio scripts and for the benefit of their own knowledge of Irish and other drama. Conversations with Criostoir O'Flynn, Seamus Heaney, and Michael Longley have also been of the greatest help to me. Finally, I am grateful to The Canada Council for their generous assistance with travel and other expenses.

* * * * * *

The following abbreviations are used:

SL   *The Saucer of Larks*
GS   *The Gold in the Sea*
Philadelphia   *Philadelphia, Here I Come!*
Cass   *The Loves of Cass McGuire*

Chronology

5 January 1929	Born Omagh, Co. Tyrone, where his father was then teaching
1939	Family moved to Derry City on father's appointment to Long Tower School
1939–1945	Educated Long Tower School and St. Columb's College, Derry
1945–48	Maynooth College, the Catholic seminary; left with B.A., but not for priesthood
1948–49	Year at home in Derry
1949–50	St. Joseph's Teacher Training College, Belfast
1950–60	Teaching in various Primary and Intermediate schools in Derry; began to write as an after-hours activity, mainly short stories, which appeared regularly in *The New Yorker* in the mid-fifties
1954	Married
1958	*A Sort of Freedom,* radio play, BBC, Northern Ireland Home Service *To This Hard House,* radio play, BBC, Northern Ireland Home Service

1959   *A Doubtful Paradise (The Francophile)*, Group Theatre, Belfast

1960   Retired from teaching to work full time as a writer

1962   *The Enemy Within*, Abbey Theatre, Dublin; BBC radio version 1963; BBC TV version 1965
        The Saucer of Larks (short stories)

1963   *The Blind Mice*, Eblana Theatre, Dublin; BBC Northern Ireland Home Service; Lyric Theatre, Belfast 1964

1964   *Philadelphia, Here I Come!* Gaiety Theatre (Dublin Theatre Festival) ; BBC radio production, 1965; Helen Hayes Theatre, New York, 1966; Lyric Theatre, London, 1967

1966   *The Gold in the Sea* (short stories)
        The Loves of Cass McGuire Helen Hayes Theatre, New York, Abbey Theatre, Dublin, 1967

1967   *Lovers* Gate Theatre, Dublin; Vivian Beaumont Theatre, New York, 1968; Fortune Theatre, London, 1969

1968   *Crystal and Fox* Gaiety Theatre, Dublin, Mark Taper Forum, Los Angeles, 1970

1969   *The Mundy Scheme* Olympia Theatre, Dublin, Royal Theatre, New York

1971   *The Gentle Island* Olympia Theatre, Dublin, Lyric Theatre, Belfast, 1972

1973   *The Freedom of the City* Abbey Theatre, Dublin, Royal Court Theatre, London

Brian Friel

1
Background and Themes: The Short Stories

I

Brian Friel's "Johnny and Mick" (SL) is a story about two boys wandering the streets of a Northern Irish town. They roam from the central Diamond, "where black soldiers of the War Memorial towered in taut menace above them," along "the brown stagnant water" of the quays, past "a mountain of scrap metal," by empty, echoing sheds, and "the rusted track" of the railway to the complacent suburbs. A suburban street is a challenge to them. It slopes down, "as wide as three ordinary streets," with its vivid gardens, soft lawns, and "careful curtains," to the river—which here "lay cool and sparkling at its feet."

They skylark, shout, disrupt the respectable stillness. A frail old man from one of the houses buys for his grandson, a childish replica of himself, the chestnuts

that Johnny and Mick have gathered. Johnny sees a
prospect of wealth. The two boys collect a great pile
of chestnuts to sell to the effete children of these
houses. Mick, trying to jump the pile, scatters it, and
the two of them frolic down the road, kicking the
chestnuts in all directions. By the river they sober up
and wordlessly set off for their Tintown squatters'
homes, where "they said the briefest of goodbyes to
one another and parted."

Their afternoon has made them aware, inarticulately,
of social division and of their own impotence. The
river, as the images discreetly imply, sets apart the
two worlds of town and suburb. Even its own waters
alter with the viewpoint. The town is decaying, moribund; the suburban road opulent, well-groomed, secure,
"a long distance from" Tintown. Johnny's life has
taught him a precocious knowingness—"look the policeman or probation officer straight in the eye and smile."
He is contemptuous of "soft guys with money," of
little boys, wearing unnecessary overcoats, who can't
climb their own trees. But he is vulnerable, as with
his chestnut scheme, to the "chill voice" of the middle
class. He and his plans exist only as a momentary con-
venience or a passing vexation. It is not all malice or
hardheartedness. The old man is innocuous, doting. But
the two worlds are worlds apart. Johnny and Mick are
the losers, though there may be a resilience that will
sustain them.

The author's role is unobtrusive. His words project
this or that image of a setting, give the dialogue its
tone and resolution, control the transitions of scene

and mood. The details consolidate themselves into the story's statement. The two rivers in one, the contrasting silences of town and suburb, the chestnuts Johnny and Mick sensuously revel in and the chestnuts the old man buys, Johnny's patronage of Mick and their final shared abashment: these are left to speak for themselves. The statement they make is Friel's, but not by explicit declaration. The voice is personal, but assimilated to its material, setting up inferences in scene and action. It is the novelist's only sort of "objectivity": "Johnny and Mick" has all the power that its reticence can confer.

The story has a strong social attachment, not narrowly political, but sensitive to the quality of individual life in a particular community. Its representativeness depends upon its realizing a distinctive, individual situation. The setting here is in fact precisely identifiable. The topography of the fictional town is close to that of Derry City, in Northern Ireland. There, Ferryquay Street leads to the Diamond and War Memorial, to Shipquay Street and the quays, and, across the river Foyle (unnamed in the story), there is a Browning Drive, though the "Browning Drive" of the story is in a different part of town, its model being Duncreggan Road with its Mature Detached Residences. More fundamental, the shaping of "Johnny and Mick" registers Friel's deep sense of Derry's divided community, though it is not restrictively about Derry.

This is the only one of the stories to take as its subject the town where Brian Friel lived for twenty-seven years. No doubt it may be argued that its identification has the interest mainly of autobiography or even just gossip. Change the street names and the story's effect would not diminish. It is important, though, as a fairly direct indication of the way in which Friel's work reaches back, however obliquely, into personal experience. Its roots are in observation and knowledge of his own region, the northwestern counties of Ireland.

II

Brian Friel now lives a few miles outside Derry, in the village of Muff, County Donegal, over the Irish Border in the Republic. He also has a cottage near Kincasslagh on the west Donegal coast, where he spends most of the summer. It is by a small, beautiful beach, and on a fine day could be the Glennafuiseog of "The Saucer of Larks." The setting of *Philadelphia, Here I Come!* is a fusion of Kincasslagh and Glenties. Friel's main family associations are with Derry, the home of his grandfather and father; and, through his mother, who was born in Glenties, with Donegal. His wife too is from Derry, and the Friels both went to school there, as do their children now.

Since his success as a dramatist, Friel has traveled widely, in the United States in particular, though not for long periods. He has remained intimate with his upbringing and his locality. He shows no desire to leave them for the cosmopolitan world of international theater. Friel's reason is not any sense of superiority. He admires and likes the actors and producers who bring his plays to the stage. He enjoys conversation, company at home, and the friendship especially of many of the Irish writers who are his contemporaries. Simply, he stays put for the continuing contact with the scenes, the characters, the circumstances that absorb his imagination.

Irish writers have a nomadic tradition. Friel has not shared this, though he had the additional motive for departure of being a Catholic in Northern Ireland, and understandably hostile to its Government's notion of democratic rule. He is one of the Northern minority, which in his native city is the more keenly aware of minority treatment because there it is in numbers a majority. Friel's father was a Nationalist member of the (now suspended) City Corporation, and Friel was himself brought up in the traditional Nationalist assumptions.

On the whole these did not produce much more by way of policies than the ideal of uniting Ireland. Anti-British sentiment was still a lively impulse. When, at the age of ten, he returned with his family to Derry in 1939, Friel says, "We believed that Germany was right and England was wrong, that sort of thing" (Eavan Boland, "The Northern Writer's Crisis of Conscience," in *The Irish Times,* 12, 13, 14 August 1970). The Northern Nationalist Party grew out of the domestic ruptures over the 1921 Treaty (and subsequent Civil War), which established the Irish Free State and in effect ratified the separate existence of Northern Ireland. As Northern Ireland opted out of a united Ireland, so did the Nationalist Party, as a parliamentary opposition, opt out of Northern Ireland. Every election became a plebiscite on partition. The Northern government had no more to do than stage-manage the victories, which weight of numbers—and where necessary gerrymandering—had made inevitable.

In these orthodox loyalties and animosities, the politics of Northern Ireland stagnated. The normally recognized poles of Left and Right found no accommodation. Socially, the two religious groups went each its own way. Even holiday patterns were symptomatic. Derry Protestants went to the seaside towns of Portrush and Portstewart. Catholics went to Donegal or elsewhere in the South. Both would stay, if at all possible, in hotels or boarding-houses owned by someone of their own faith.

The controls exerted by these almost ritualistic observances disquieted Friel. He has been fully conscious of the dismal record of almost all clerics of all the churches, his own included. His favorite "thin book" is *My Contribution to Ecumenism* by—a dignitary of the Catholic Church in the North. As well as the many delinquencies of the Protestant majority, he recognizes the Catholic suspicion of any enterprise— not that many were offered—designed to bring together people of different faiths. A "little theatre" begun in Derry in the late 1940s languished, and soon foundered, at least partly on that distrust. Friel is a practicing Catholic. But he found his Maynooth experience "very disturbing," and his writings, when they touch on the Church and its servants, are far from reverential. He has offended not only Unionist, but Nationalist and Catholic, sensibilities.

It was in the mid-1960s that the Civil Rights movement set out systematically to disturb both traditions of thought. Like all Northern writers, Friel has often been asked to pronounce on the political upheaval that has followed. Until *The Freedom of the City* he has never taken it, or for that matter old-style Northern politics, directly as a subject. But it is worth consideration here. It epitomizes in a particularly brutal and revealing way the division that is an inescapable part of Friel's inheritance. It has compelled him to examine his responsibilities as a writer in circumstances that increasingly drive loyalties to extremes, to riot and killing. It was exactly in the Derry of "Johnny and Mick" that these things happened.

The Civil Rights Movement in Northern Ireland has from the start been far from homogeneous. It included moderate reformers, like John Hume in Derry, who hoped to unite people on a nonsectarian basis around a few straightforward issues like religious discrimination in housing, or the undemocratic franchise for local government elections. In its early days it won some Protestant support. The first and very considerable show of unity was over the location of the second Northern Irish university, which went not to Derry but to the more generally Protestant district of Coleraine. On more overtly political issues, perhaps fifty Protestants joined the Derry Civil Rights march of 5 October 1968, which was first banned and then, when the ban was defied, used for a display of police force. The movement also undoubtedly attracted many Catholics who were anti-Unionist in a perfectly orthodox Nationalist sense. Bernadette Devlin has recalled how in Enniskillen the organizers of a Civil Rights march found their supporters more interested in singing "Papish" songs than "We shall Overcome." She, with Michael Farrell, and Eamonn McCann of Derry, represented another district entity in the Civil Rights Association, the People's Democracy.

Their premises were specifically Marxist. They assented to the tactic of peaceful demonstration, but looked beyond particular grievances to the power structures that, in their view, kept the poor divided. Consequently they opened up terms of reference that were quite novel, though they did hark back to the United Irishmen of 1798, and more nearly to James Connolly's model of an Irish Socialist Republic.

But it was less the radical ideas of the 1916 rebels than simply their martyrdom that brought Irish independence closer. Left-wing activism is an exotic growth in Irish politics. Its hold is narrow and tenuous. In Derry in the 1970 General Election for one of the seats at Westminster, the Unionist won as usual. Of the two opposition candidates to him, Eamonn McCann ran a bad second to Eddie MacAteer, who with the support of John Hume stood as a "Unity" candidate, but had been for many years the Nationalist Party M.P. in the Belfast Parliament. The votes that in the same election returned Bernadette Devlin to Parliament were, with perhaps a few bizarre exceptions, Catholic votes.

Certainly, while the Civil Rights Association held briefly together, its People's Democracy members con-tributed positively to pushing a reluctant Government into either measures of reform or the promise of them. But like most small Left-wing movements, the People's Democracy proved highly fissile. Since its first successes, the Civil Rights Association has fragmented, in part at least because of leadership and doctrinal squabbles within the People's Democracy. Neither the movement as a whole nor any of its components has extinguished habits of response made almost instinctive by tradition and upbringing. Indeed, a commentator from the Republic, John Feeney, has argued that the main effect of Civil Rights activity has been to impede nonsectarian cooperation within the Labour Party and the Trade Unions (*The Irish Times*, 15, 16 September 1970). A moderate Northern observer, Martin Wallace, points out that, whatever the reforms, "the bulk of the power will rest with the Protestant majority," and the prospect of beneficial results from reform legislation has dwindled because Protestant attitudes "have hardened as leadership of the Catholic minority has tended to pass from civil rights moderates to more extreme republicans intent on bringing down the government" ("Reform in the North," *Eire-Ireland*, Autumn 1970).

Protestants are easily persuaded that the C.R.A. cloaked a combination of simple Republicanism and anti-Protestantism—the precise converse of their own sectarian attitudes—with some Maoist/Marxist (international) subversion thrown in for good measure. Catholics continue to distrust Protestants. Working-class unity remains an ideal, not a fact. Pointless violence continues. Inherited hatreds persist. The conventions

the political turmoil their subject. *Hibernia's* "News in the Arts" (28 August 1970) has hinted at the need for an even larger zeal. Recalling Brecht's procrastination in the 1953 Berlin uprising—"the rebellion went down to defeat with the artist sitting by his tape-recorder, inglorious, unbloody, uninvolved"—the columnist adds, rather enigmatically, "a clear message for the artist in Ireland today, North and South." A month later in the same journal, Maurice Leitch urges exactly the opposite view, that such admonitions are impertinent, for the "situation . . . if [writers] are to be honest to themselves and to their work, must be folded away into the brain for some sort of ripening process to take place."

Writers have in fact turned their craft to the subject. Seamus Heaney's "Docker" was published in 1966, before the violence became commonplace. Though it regards its subject with wit, it is plainly conscious of a perpetual menace:

> That fist would drop a hammer on a Catholic—
> Oh, yes, that kind of thing could start again;
> The only Roman collar he tolerates
> Smiles all round his sleek pint of porter.

John Boyd's *The Assassin* was produced with great impact at the 1969 Dublin Theatre Festival. It is a powerful, Brechtian treatment of the political murder of a Northern Protestant agitator, its dark causes and bloody sequel.

At a less consequential level, the Peacock Theatre presented, in September 1970, *A State of Chassis,* described as "a political-polemical-satirical review," written by a Northerner, John D. Stewart, and two Southerners, Thomas MacAnna and Eugene Walters, and dealing with people and events in Northern Ireland. At the first night, Eamonn McCann demonstrated against its "trivialisation" of serious issues—players "jumping around for the delectation of the people of Dublin who can afford 17s.6d. a seat" (*Irish Times* report, 17 September, 1970). The Northern Opposition M.P.s who were present, though less vehement, also found the piece offensive. Two months later Mr. McCann, opening an Exhibition by a student of the Dublin College of Art, explained his view of the artist's role. He commended the student whose works were on exhibition because he was politically involved in a dispute at the College of Art, and another student for his involvement in the cement workers' strike. "No art," he said, "is neutral." Its only defensible function is "to contribute to the struggle of the people against exploitation" (*ibid.,* 4 November 1970).

So rigidly doctrinaire a view is unacceptable to Friel, though he has, inevitably, considered the schism and its bitterness as a possible subject. One problem has been the form that for him would best express it. He has ceased to write short stories; he finds neither Boyd's Brechtian theatre nor Stewart's satirical revue appropriate to himself; and he is in any case suspicious of a theme or subject that does not generate its own answer to the question of form.

As long ago as 1965 (in *Acorn,* Magee College Derry, Spring 1965), Friel repudiated crusading art and plays designed, like Osborne's or Wesker's, to put across a social message. The writer's job is rather to present "a set of people and a situation with a certain clarity and understanding and sympathy and as a result of this one should look at them more closely; and if one is moved then that one should react accordingly. This is the responsibility of a reader or an audience, but I don't think it's the writer's." Nevertheless, Friel recognizes fine distinctions. Though it should not be the writer's end purpose, his work may admit to an audience's mind a response, an illumination, that may, sometime, lead to action. And the writer has his arrogance. This is how things are, he is saying, with the expectation that his audience will concur.

Since then, Friel has applied these principles to his own circumstances. A basic impediment to his taking a Northern political subject is that he is "emotionally too much involved about it"; and the situation itself "is in transition at the moment." A play on this theme "will not be written," he hopes, "for another ten or fifteen years" ("The Future of Irish Drama," *The Irish Times,* 12 February 1970). In a later interview he has elaborated, and perhaps somewhat modified, these propositions. He recalls a demonstration about housing in Derry, "before the big burst." "I happened to be in it," he comments, "not because I was involved, but because I was an interested spectator at that point." Subsequently, he took up the idea of the artist as spectator:

Graham Greene has said that every writer is like a housewife who won't discard a piece of string in case she may

use it. The crisis is there, and I keep wondering how it
can be of use to me. I know this may seem a very selfish
attitude. But it is, after all, a professional approach to the
situation. On a personal level, of course, we're all terribly
involved in it. But for the writer, I think his position is
better as a sideline one, as against an involved one. This
is against the feeling of the moment where writers every-
where are becoming more and more committed socially.
(Boland)

On the personal level he refers to, Friel has con-
tributed to what little is being done to enlighten mu-
tual incomprehension. He has persistently urged on
the Northern Ireland Arts Council the need for a
"National Theatre," preferably located outside Belfast.
In March 1970 he adjudicated a drama festival presented by the four Derry grammar schools, two Catholic
and two Protestant. In 1970/71, he arranged and took
part in a series of lectures and seminars given by
distinguished Irish writers and performers at the University College in Derry—Presbyterian founded, now
an appendage of the New University at Coleraine. Elsewhere, but not in Northern Ireland, these activities
would not be cause for special comment.

Professionally, Friel still gives precedence to the literary craft and its autonomous ends. Friel does hold
that an artist is all the better for a viewpoint, whether
it be Communist, Catholic, Civil Rights, or whatever,
so long as he can avoid any factional association. He
has no desire, in a situation characterized by flux, to
be identified with, for example, a traditional Nation-
alist/Catholic policy line, and was disturbed by the
Hume/McAteer electoral alliance in Derry. But Friel

quite rightly believes that his opinions, and the very fact of having opinions, place no obligation on him to import them directly into his work. "People keep insisting," he has said to the present writer,

> why don't you write a play about Civil Rights, Biafra, the Bomb, the Arms Trial . . . the Disappearance of the Small Family Grocer, Smoking and Lung Cancer, etc. etc. And when I explain that it seems to me that such a request implies a confusion of the artist's and the journalist's function I'm told I'm not "of my time." (May I exclude the Small Family Grocer. He sounds minutely interesting.) In other words I know of no Irish writer who is not passionately engaged in our current problems. But he must maintain a perspective as a writer, and— equally important—he will write about the situation in terms that may not relate even remotely to the squalor of here and now.

Other writers have made a similar point.

Seamus Heaney, Michael Longley and Derek Mahon have all spoken of how the Northern situation may have a kind of subterranean presence in works that ostensibly have nothing to do with it. Mahon recognizes even in some love poems "metaphors for the Northern situation" taken from quite private dilemmas. More particularly, Heaney cites his poem, "The Last Mummer." It portrays this representative of a dying art parading the suburbs, angry with frustration, and throwing stones at the houses. "I didn't," Heaney comments, "mean this to be a poem about Northern Ireland, but in some way I think it is" (Boland) .

Some such formula accounts for Friel's assimilation to his work of the social and political strain in his background. He is not out to convey a social message, still less to incite political action. "Johnny and Mick" is unusual in allowing that sort of inference. Even there it is, so to speak, the emotional premises, not a political conclusion, that the story states.

"The Potato Gatherers" (SL) is perhaps rather the same. Early on a freezing November morning two young boys set out to help a farmer dig his potatoes. But despite the day off from school—which will be paid for in punishment—and the prospect of spending what they earn, their excitement stales in the bitter cold: " . . . their bodies shuddered with pain and the tall trees reeled and the hedges rose to the sky." At the end of the day they are left the one forlornly clinging to his hopes, the other sullen in exhaustion.

The point is not that the story acquires political substance because it is about the children of a poor family. But it unquestionably embodies social comment. It is in the sense of loss, of humble pleasures flawed, so intimately bound in with the images: of the tractor's sound broken off against the cold air and "drumming at the back of [Philly's] eyes," of the hard clay, encaging landscape, motionless sky—images of constriction and inflexibility, which are an image of one disposition in a society, and of a response to it. The stories uncover other dispositions too, and of a kinder sort. They create a variety of relationships between their fictional world and its counterparts in reality. In their themes and images is the spirit of the place, the quality of experience that led to confrontation in the streets. Friel's stories of the people and the places he knows remark the whole of which this is a part.

III

The "real" world of Brian Friel's short stories reaches from Kincasslagh in the west of Donegal through Strabane, Derry City, and Coleraine to Omagh and County Tyrone. Alongside, at times superimposed on, these actual places are the imagined towns, villages, and country districts—Beannafreaghan, Glennafuiseog, Corradinna, Mullaghduff. These are composites and extensions of reality, given substance by an intense receptiveness to the atmosphere of a day or season, to the run of landscape, the play of light and shade, all the tangibles that localize a time and place. The vibrant solidity of the settings is perhaps the strongest single impression left by the world of these stories, memorable because never merely a background décor.

In "The Saucer of Larks" (SL), the scene is the story's impulse. Landscape, mood, and human feeling are inseparably mixed. The place is Donegal. Two men from the German War Graves Commission, guided by the local Sergeant and Guard, have come to remove the body of a wartime pilot, buried where he crashed on an Atlantic promontory, to the official graveyard.

It is a spring morning, "with the sea spreading out and away into a warm sky and a high, fresh sun taking winking lights out of the granite-covered countryside." The grave is in Glennafuiseog, where a hill cuts off the sea breeze and "they heard the larks, not a couple or a dozen or a score, but hundreds of them, all invisible against the blue heat of the sky, an umbrella of music over this tiny world below." Under this Arcadian colour and tranquility, the land's harsher foundation remains: "obdurate, peaty, rocky earth," "barren bogland," "an occasional gnarled tree."

Something in the scene and their errand precipitates in the Sergeant recognition of an elegiac appropriateness in "being buried out here in the wilds." Shocking himself, he suggests that they leave the dead airman where he lies, but the Germans go methodically about their business, while "the emptiness was filled again by the larks, slowly at first, then more and more of them until the saucer-valley shimmered with their singing."

The party returns to the police station. The Sergeant cautions Guard Burke to keep his mouth shut about this aberration and walks to his office, "for a man of his years and shape . . . with considerable dignity."

Glennafuiseog combines three or four real places and a particular kind of day. As the story fuses them, they move beyond reality to express what the Sergeant cannot quite find words for—he "was not too sure that he had made himself clear." But it is not only the description—so economically evocative of heat, of an indomitable solitude, of rest—that works to this end. The Sergeant's lamer words have their own colloquial eloquence. They counterpoint the lyrical descriptive passages, the Germans' matter-of-fact orderliness, Guard Burke's stolidity. The Sergeant is the focus; it is the scene that most fully voices his half-apprehended feelings of loss and sanctuary.

Like the Sergeant, the protagonists of these stories often have very strongly the feeling that they are of a piece with a place. They are, however, anything but creatures of circumstance. The kinship between man and place may satisfy because it has the assurance of familiarity. But the familiarity may be harsh, demanding; and it is inexhaustible, liable always to disclose unsuspected outlines. There is a process of learning and readjustment. The individual remains his own man.

In "The Flower of Kiltymore" (GS), old Sergeant Burke, having one day neglected his duty more through the fault of others than himself, is saddled with the blame for a local disaster. Oddly, the disgrace gets rid of an emptiness in his recent life. Since the death of his thwarted, scoffing wife he had been ignored by his village tormentors, the "Blue Boys," a wild set of rapscallions, who played vicious enough tricks on him. Now in his humiliation they hound him again—he has killed "the flower of Kiltymore."

Their renewed attentions are not unwelcome. They are part of the life ended by his wife's death, the life of courtship, marriage, hopes, childlessness and modest ambitions disappointed, of the Blue Boys' mindless abuse. It might seem a life fitly represented by the lone tree in Burke's garden, "a frail trunk, and agonized leafless branches that leaned away from the barracks . . . as if they were appealing for comfort." But on the day of the disaster Sergeant Burke welcomes its renewal of "so many familiar things." He knows he can endure. His "life had suddenly, happily, slipped back into its old groove."

The Sergeant is a "failure," certainly a butt. No one takes him seriously. Yet through all his humiliations, like his exchanges with his gleefully mocking Guard, he keeps within himself a dignity that nothing can violate. The story achieves the difficult transitions from comic to tragic. "Mr. Sing My Heart's Delight," (SL) with a more purely comic emphasis, exuberantly displays another facet of the will to endure, in circumstances that seem likelier to extinguish it.

The narrator recalls his annual winter visits as a child to his Grandmother's one-room house, deep in Donegal, while his Grandfather worked in Scotland. The story has links with the Rabelaisian tradition of Irish writing. Granny's daughter, the narrator's mother, was not the child of Grandfather. Now, secluded in the wilds by a possessive husband, Granny's prodigal spirit survives in a free but innocent swearing and a boisterous vitality, singing, dancing, running the moor, romancing about the liners that pass the coast: "Lords and Ladies," she would say. "The men of them handsome and straight as heroes and the women of them in bright silks down to their toes and all of them laughing and dancing and drinking wine and singing."

The cheap wares brought one day by an Indian packman, whom she christens "Mr. Sing my heart's delight," stimulate her dreams of exotic lands and people. She gives him food and lodging for the night, and when he leaves he presents her with his ring, "now black, now blood red, now blue, now the colour of sloes in the August sun." She thinks compassionately of his life on this alien soil, "rocky, barren, uneven, covered by a brown heather that never blooms"; and of her own life too. She is in a way an alien spirit herself, in her extravagant fancies unlike the region. Yet she is also of the place and its stark beauty, like the "wild geese spearing through the icy air high above the ocean." Her imagination and her generosity are part of it.

It is a complex story, full of images of flight, passage and the home, exile and communion. It is also about experience recalled, the adult now seeing fully what had eluded the child. Many of the stories turn upon reminiscences of childhood, and in a variety of ways. "Among the Ruins" (SL) returns a family for a day to Corradinna, where the father spent his childhood holidays. Tempers fray; the day goes sour, reducing his past to illusion. But finally, after the day's fluidly shifting moods and alliances, his memories are reasserted as in the tender conclusion he recalls his own son's fancies that day, "donging the tower":

> magic and sustenance in the brief, quickly destroyed happiness of their children. The past did have meaning. It was neither reality nor dreams, neither today's patchy oaks nor the great woods of his boyhood. It was simply continuance, life repeating itself and surviving.

Past and present interact here, each endorsing the truth of the other, which it had threatened to deny.

Elsewhere, more like "Mr. Sing," the past takes shape

within a present that makes no real entrance into the story. Such are "The Illusionists" (GS) and "My Father and the Sergeant" (SL). Both narrators look back to a boyhood as the son of the Principal of an insignificant primary school in County Tyrone, the first some miles from Omagh, the second in "Knockenagh." Though some of the detail does overlap, their histories are distinct.

M. L'Estrange, an itinerant conjurer, makes a yearly visit to the school where Mr. Boyle is Principal. Each visit follows a pattern of oddly capricious emotion, conveyed early in the story by a narrative montage of the habitual events. To the children, L'Estrange is "the most wonderful man in the world." Boyle is the impresario, genial, enthusiastic, but growing morose and in the end insulting the conjurer, both of them by then half drunk. To Mrs. Boyle, L'Estrange is "that old trickster." During his performance the class is rapt, the father "relaxed and smooth with content," L'Estrange seedily elegant, enacting his routine with "soft, sad eyes" and "tired smile."

The story describes his last visit, when young Boyle had secretly decided to run off as an assistant magician with L'Estrange. In a marvelously comic scene the two men pursue their antiphonal monologues. Each is his own hero in a world where wishing has made it so. L'Estrange has been the darling of cosmopolitan audiences, Boyle's integrity has held him loyal, against a thousand temptations, to his ramshackle school. Around them, mother and son go about the work of the home.

In their conclusive quarrel the two mock each other's self-deceptions. The boy's final disillusionment is to find L'Estrange grandiloquently drunk in the bleak night, lying beside his bicycle, his gimcrack props, his torpid rabbit. The mother comforts her son with memories of their summer pastimes. In her conviction of happiness he recognizes truth. It is the truth of hard knocks, tedious chores, and their easement in living pleasures, against the vexatious dreams of the two illusionists. The story's opening phase formulates the pattern and glances at its eventual disintegration in the second. Its structure precisely reflects the boy's own movement into clearer recognition of the world he really lives in, which does not exclude compassion for the two old losers.

Mr. Hargan, Principal of Knockenagh Elementary School, is both "my father" and "the Sergeant" (his nickname) of the title. His career resembles Mr. Boyle's —early success and then a career in the same deteriorating backwater school, "served by one dry toilet whose stale odour lay heavy on our playground."

Hargan has hung onto reality more tenaciously than Boyle. Instead of celebrating imaginary triumphs he sets himself to coaching four pupils, among them his son, to win regional scholarships, "troubled by an ambition I never understood until years later." We never learn the outcome of this, nor is it important. The story's issue is the critical turns in human relationships, not just contrived narrative suspense.

Joe sees his father as two quite distinct people—the kindly, taciturn parent, and the rigid, autocratic "Sergeant." Though in a way confusing, keeping the two isolated each in his own sphere is a practical working arrangement. Here too, events disrupt the pattern. Hargan has the minor victory of being needed in and answering to a crisis. The pattern is restored, at least in its externals. The school is its drab self, the instruction dry as ever. Hargan is unchanged. But, however briefly, Joe has seen his father and "the Sergeant" as one, and perhaps, in this new perspective, begun the process, consummated "years later," of understanding him.

This story, unlike the almost claustrophobic "The Illusionists," places the family situation firmly out in the surrounding life of Knockenagh. For Joe, his father is one concern among a myriad others that the story keeps before us. It does not finish with any neat reckoning of an isolated experience. The reader's strongest impression is of interlocked circumstances working their untidy way to open up fresh views of accepted and familiar associations.

Both these are stories of crisis recollected from childhood, of a moment or a sequence of events that refashioned attitudes and feelings, though acquiring definition only in much later retrospect. In "Foundry House" (SL), "a vague deference to something long ago"—certain childhood relationships—impregnates and influences the present, in which the main action takes place.

Derry City, remotely, furnishes the scene. Outside the town is Victoria Park, a residential area, wooded, stretching from a hillside to the main Derry-Strabane road and the river, in the story "a million momentary flashes of light that danced and died in the vegetation." On the riverbank stood an attractive little railway station (now a spirit warehouse), which becomes the foundry of the story. It is a place that can be quite evocative of "something long ago." In a setting like this, Joe Brennan encounters the sadness of old age, separation, and decay.

He has come back with his family to the gate lodge, where his father had lived as an employee, then a pensioner, of Hogan's foundry. Mrs. Hogan of Foundry House remembers Joe from the youth of her children, Declan and Claire, both now in religious orders. Mr. Hogan, whom Joe recalls as "a large, stern-faced man with a long white beard and a heavy step and a walking stick," is a useful bogeyman for the Brennan children, though he is never seen. In this situation, on an October evening "uneasy with cold breezes," Mrs. Hogan calls to ask if Joe will bring a tape-recorder to play a message from Claire, who will never come back from her mission in Africa.

At the door of the Hogan house, Joe remembers taking messages there from the foundry in his boyhood. This is his first time to enter. Father Declan, professionally effusive, welcomes him and, when the recorder is installed in the dilapidated breakfast room, brings down his father. He is a great ruin of a man, a "huge, monolithic figure that inched its way across the faded carpet . . . his face, fleshy, trembling, coloured in dead purple and gray-black . . . the eyes, wide and staring and quick with the terror of stumbling."

Claire's recorded message, grotesquely ironic, is addressed to the house she knew, imagining her parents as they were in the now-abandoned drawing room. In her memory they still go about affairs long beyond their powers or interest. Finally she plays an old tune on her violin. Wordless since his entrance, Mr. Hogan, "the veins in his neck dilating, the mouth shaping in preparation for speech," calls out his daughter's name and collapses in his chair. Having helped put Mr. Hogan to bed, Joe is left alone downstairs and goes home without either farewell or the tape-recorder.

A brief sequel, with Joe back at home, returns to the framework opened at the beginning. It avoids interpretation. We have impersonal stage directions, dialogue, no more. Quizzed by his wife, Joe is unresponsive. Claire's message was "lovely," and "they loved it"; Father Declan is "a fine man. A fine priest"; Mr. Hogan, though older, "unchanged"; the house "lovely," "beautiful." Caressing the newest baby, Joe "crooned into the child's ear, "A great family. A grand family." He means the Hogans. The reader, undistracted by the stirred-up sediment of memories, is aware of more intricate responses than Joe will utter.

There is a theatrical quality in the story's main scene, with the ritualized family gathering, the disembodied voice of the tape-recorder, the old man's gruesome entrance, and his seizure bringing about the collective exit. These histrionic effects embody the highly charged emotions that flicker through the scene. We are seeing it as it strikes Joe, responsive to his memories and the accumulating tensions of past and present coming together.

Friel is speaking almost entirely through the events. We have only what we see and hear to go by. There is no commentary on what the characters think and feel, and in this way too the mode of presentation has the character of drama. Friel has himself spoken of underwriting as a fault in his work. He means a reluctance to clinch by express comment a motive or a conclusion. "Foundry House" is one of the stories in which the "omniscient author" is wariest of declaring his access to the unspoken.

In a way, the story transplants a familiar tradition in Irish writing, tales of "the Big House," especially in its decline. The priest in Sean O'Faolain's "A Broken World," all his life hostile to the planter gentry, feels in their departure almost a bereavement, private and communal: "they in their octagon and we in our lighted cabins, I mean to say, it was two halves of a world." Even the narrator, impatient of Irish lethargy, cannot "deny to the wintry moment its own truth." Similarly in "Lord and Master," also by O'Faolain, the old schoolteacher finally recognizes between himself and Lord Carew, within their conflict, a sympathy of interest. In these two stories the Big House, envied, detested, is yet in its decay an object of regret, a relic of the Anglo-Irish achievement, uneasily detached from and intimate with Irish life. There is perhaps a hint of the relationship in Friel's "Everything Neat and Tidy" (GS), set in County Tyrone,

where, although people of substance, the "MacMena-
mins never had the wealth or the position of Lady
Hartnell of Killard."

But "Foundry House" does not grow out of the
long and complex traffic between Gaelic Ireland and
Anglo Ireland. The afflictions of its Big House are
more personal than social and historical. The Hogans
are Northern Catholic bourgeois; Joe Brennan is an
artisan. Though their lives are separate, they have a
more homogeneous world in common.

Friel's regional background and his period give him
a quite different point of departure from that of O'Faolain's squireens and peasants. Yet the story produces
similar perceptions of past working into present, of
waning life, and the prospect of new growth. For all
its melancholy, "Foundry House," like "Among the
Ruins," leaves as its final impression, "continuance,
life repeating itself and surviving."

It is an arduous survival. Adversity, self-deception,
illusion, are the constant challenges in the homogeneous
world that knits together even from this selection from
the stories. We are not in the stereotyped Ireland of
holy peasants and farcical roisterers. Defeated, or clinging to reality, the characters have the perplexed hu-
manity that earns them Friel's compassion. Though
they will not confess, they may recognize, their own
illusions, which do not supplant reality but make it
tolerable.

Con, in "The Gold in the Sea" (GS), knows the
rough life and meager rewards of a Donegal small
farmer/part-time fisherman. Voluble, ebullient, he sets

off with his partners, Philly his nephew, and Lispy, on. the fishing trip the story describes. The main sequence is antiphonal dialogue, authentic and inventively comic, the idiom unfaked. Con recounts legends of his travels, and of the bullion in the sea under their boat, left when the *Boniface* was sunk there in 1917. From time to time Philly corrects him, without conviction. Lispy throws in his inconsequential proverbs. They net six fish. Now tired, old-looking, Con admits to the narrator that the gold in the sea, if it was ever there, has long been salvaged. He keeps up the pretense for the sake of Philly and Lispy—"they never got much out of life. Not like me."

It is as much if not more his own pretense, though not cherished like the travels he so embroiders. Sensing his need for assurance, the narrator affirms Con's eminence as a traveled man. The lies are harmless ones, necessary to Con. They are his release from hard work and poverty. More important, they represent a vigor and an imaginative vitality whose truth he can speak only through his tall tales. Con is not a refugee from facts. At the end, a new story is clearly flowering in his mind. With it, his strength for life is returning, and as he has asserted earlier, "By God, there'll be another day," and "The fish is there."

The realities of Con's life are subsistence farming and parish horizons, romantic to the tourist, but for the locals meaning drudgery and, often, little-minded parochialism. This parochialism figures in the Ireland of these stories, along with its aging bachelors and outnumbered women. It has its share of stifling respectability, ever ready to be outraged or titillated. At the end of "The Diviner" (GS), Nelly Doherty weeps because she has not lived down her first husband's drunken escapades and established "a foothold on respectability."

Nelly's second husband, apparently "the acme of respectability," has lived quietly with her for three months. They keep themselves to themselves. Then, before the whole village, he is found drowned in the lake, with two whiskey bottles in his pockets, and the masquerade collapses. The diviner, brought from outside the county, in locating the body also brings its secret to light. The story is not, as many scenes in *Philadelphia* are, corrosively satirical of village life. It does not lampoon the villagers. All of them act generously; and they see the reason for Nelly's tears—not only because of "twenty-five years of humility and mortification but, more bitter still, tears for the past three months, when appearances had almost won." Yet, within the conditions of "respectability" imposed by the village, Nelly's "happiness" (keeping up appearances) is not much preferable to her misery.

"The Highwayman and the Saint" (GS), set in Omagh, is more mordant about small-town prudery and sanctimoniousness. Madge Wilson's invalided mother has two interests in life. The first is her reverence for St. Philomena, whose shrine dominates her bedroom. The second is ringing her hand-bell to interrupt the courting on the living-room couch between her daughter and Andy, the narrator. To avoid suspicious silences, Andy recites "The Highwayman," while

Madge throws in occasional snatches of small talk. But the tactic has no great success. The courting is less regular than nightly prayers in Mrs. Wilson's bedroom.

Eventually they marry, but go to live in the Wilson home, not the house Andy has bought. Madge's resentment against her mother mysteriously diminishes. The crisis is Andy's discovery that the Vatican has forbidden devotions to St. Philomena, who may never have existed. He gets drunk and gives the news to Mrs. Wilson. Madge becomes her mother's ally and Mrs. Wilson —"her face was white and sad and holy looking"— selects a new (and secret) saint for her devotions. Andy ends up like the late Mr. Wilson, defeated, spending his leisure sheltered behind the old man's unnecessary binoculars, bird-watching in the tiny garden of the Wilson house.

Some of the comedy is broad and boisterous. Andy accompanies his denunciation of St. Philomena by the fifteenth verse of "The Highwayman," a kind of secular replacement for the Rosary normally recited in the bedroom. "The family that prays together stays together" becomes for him, "The family that thinks together drinks together." Friel is devastating in his observation of ready-made devotional platitudes. Here they happen to be Catholic, but they have their dour counterparts in any religion practiced in the North of Ireland. Friel's target is not faith, but a faith whose observance is mechanical, outward, self-righteous.

The one-act play "Losers," based on the story, makes hilarious use of this lifeless canting in the really hair-raising unctuousness of Mrs. Wilson and her neighbor.

But despite the comedy, the events are ultimately depressing, and even more so in the story, where humor, however astringent, has a less conspicuous part. Andy is a victim of the war, Irish style, between the sexes and between the aged and the middle-aged; of the genteel pretensions of an old-maidish religion. It is a situation commonly enough taken up by Irish writers, from Joyce's "The Boarding House" to O'Faolain's "Childybawn" and Brian Moore's *The Feast of Lupercal*. The subject does not, then, have a peculiarly regional origin. But the place of religion in Friel's writings does have regional implications.

The environment of his stories is a Catholic one. He is not an artist of the whole community, Protestant and Catholic. It is likely impossible that he could be. So widely are the two groups set apart by different school systems, by divergent historical loyalties, by sectarian government, that neither has any real and natural intimacy with the other. As John Cronin has argued ("Ulster's Alarming Novels," *Eire-Ireland* [Winter 1969]), none of the Northern Writers, of either persuasion, has been able to "transcend the divisions of the region," where sectarian politics thrive on the archaic enmities it is their business to foster. Yet it is also true that Friel's stories betray no least hint of rancor in their author, and, though not "political," irradiate political correspondences, in their recurring motifs of flight and exile, and the whole complex medley of the shifting alliances between man and place.

Friel's settings are mostly rural and the people he writes about poor. The discussion of the stories referred to here, only about a third of the total in the two collections, undoubtedly makes too little of their humor. However, although the characters are often hardy, spirited, and their presentation lighthearted, the tone of the stories seems to me predominantly elegiac: for loves, friendships, observances, past or fated to pass. They establish a transient but crucial mood, generated by the traffic between past and present, place and person. The moments to cherish are those that isolate the quality of a life, of a relationship with one's fellows or one's region. The participants sense rather than define their significance; and the stories' purpose is not only to state the moment but to preserve that indeterminateness. As Bernard feels at the end of "Aunt Maggie, the Strong One" (SL), knowledge "of all he had witnessed could no longer be contained in the intellect alone but was dissolving already and overflowing into the emotions." The stories too retain within themselves a core of meaning that resists paraphrase.

2
Early Plays: Private Conversation and Public Address

I

Early in 1958 the Northern Ireland BBC presented Brian Friel's *A Sort of Freedom,* a play written for radio. Its protagonist is Jack Frazer, owner of a road haulage firm. With large and eventually dishonored promises he encourages Joe Reddin, one of his employees and a friend of less prosperous days, to hold out against joining the Trade Union: "I'm a free man to do as I want."

At home, Frazer and his wife live at odds. Childless, they have just adopted an infant son, on whom Frazer lavishes a self-indulgent love. He tries, and fails, to evade an inoculation requirement for the baby ("A man should be free to choose"). By the end of the play the child has died, through an accident—"He would have been me," Frazer says. He and his wife resume their bickering. Reddin, grudgingly and ungenerously compensated for the loss of his job, retains his esteem for Frazer—"The decentest man in this town, in the whole country . . . I always knew it."

Frazer is a mean-spirited piece of work, somewhat resembling John Fibbs in George Shiels's *The Passing Day,* who is on the same rancorous terms with his wife. All Frazer's associations have the same deadly barrenness of feeling. This is really the center of the play, which, though it seems to promise the Union dispute as a "social issue," develops it rather perfunctorily. This dispute becomes instead an occasion to explore the claims of friendship and loyalty, and to disclose the hidden reaches of a relationship entirely misapprehended by Joe Reddin. The ending is ironic, discomforting. Any meaning the events might have had for Reddin is concealed from him. Frazer and his wife remain as they were at the beginning. No one ends up "a lot wiser, a little nobler, and preferably a bit sadder" (Friel, "The Theatre of Hope and Despair").

The same is true of *To This Hard House,* broadcast later in the same year. Daniel Stone, like Mr. Hargan in "My Father and the Sergeant," is watching his moribund school go under to "population trends, new industries, etc.," which have brought a modern school to the nearby town. Again the premises of the action have a broadly social character: government regulations, copiously cited by Stone, and a mobile community will decide Stone's career. But the play is not asking us to contemplate The Fate of the Rural School, or Problems of the Retired Teacher.

Stone's professional anxieties are just one precipitant in a family struggle of wills where authority and judgment are deserting the father. His children bewilder him by giving up their prescribed roles. We leave him still intent on advising his son, pettishly "forgiving" one daughter whose lover reneges on an elopement, and awaiting another who clearly will never return. Stone is abstracting himself from reality, and the mild domestic comedy of the opening gives way to the pathos of an undignified surrender.

Friel wrote these plays while he was still primarily occupied with the short story. They recall "The Illusionists," "The Flower of Kiltymore," "The Gold in the Sea," whose characters are similarly engaged in their various degrees of compromise with disappointment and the hard life. The plays, however, do not achieve their design with the authority of the stories. In both of them there is perhaps some uncertainty about their intention: whether it is to scrutinize dilemmas imposed by the larger social establishments, or to unriddle the private codes of family affections. With the disappearance, too, of the stories' narrative and description, the dialogue has to assume new obligations that it is not yet able to fulfil. There is no equivalent to the mediating voice that in the stories suggests directions of understanding and sympathy. Consequently the characters here seem more simplified and more readily sized up.

These radio plays have nevertheless the fascination, often vexing to a writer, of all early work. Though Friel disowns them, they did induce him to pursue further what they had not said to his satisfaction. He wrote his next play, *A Doubtful Paradise* (originally *The Francophile*), for the stage. It was produced in 1959 in Belfast at the "Group Theatre—before it collapsed. It was a dreadful play. I don't think the Group Company collapsed because of it, but it didn't do them any good. It was a very bad play and I like to forget about it" (*Acorn*).

Despite Friel's disenchantment now, the play is a perceptive attempt to resolve the conflicting purposes of *To This Hard House,* whose events and relationships it reworks. The later play imposes on its comparable situations a steadier line of sight. Willie Logue is acting overseer in the Derry Post Office, a man of vast but defective cultural pretensions. Dedicated in his current phase to French civilization (classes at the local Technical school), he is to be harassed by: hopes of promotion (which do not materialize); his son's disbarment; the rejection of the family by one daughter (who has "married well"); and the abortive elopement of the other with a spurious French Count, at first much venerated by Willie.

Where Stone's job, or Frazer's, has an existence independent of their personal being, and at least intimates questions of social concern, Willie's is just another circumstance in our view of him. It supplies an experience for him to embroider; it raises no issues not intrinsic to his own futility. As Mrs. Logue sees, in a

Brian Friel

bitter dialogue with her husband, their misfortunes are a consequence of Willie's years of bogus refinement: these are the locus of the play.

This is not entirely to contradict Friel's view of his play. For example, however one may query the tidy dramatic formula "problem—attack on problem—resolution of the problem," ("The Theatre of Hope and Despair"), Willie's final answer—to take up Esperanto the next winter—is not prepared for within the play, which appears to be moving him toward some practical sense. "Are you going to sign on the dole?", he asks his son; "how will you live for the next six months?" A hesitancy between farce—Willie has his genuinely funny moments—and realism may be the play's conceptual defect. Nonetheless, it is an advance on the radio plays. It has a thematic integrity; there is a sense of the past penetrating the present; and there is in Willie promise of a character given full dramatic life.

Though it was not the next to be performed, *The Blind Mice* is the next play Friel wrote. It too he considers a bad play. It is a decided attempt to locate in the world of politics a crisis of various loyalties. Father Chris Carroll, released after five years' imprisonment in Communist China, comes home a hero. The Bishop is to visit. The townsfolk plan a parade—"There'll be a riot," says Carroll's father, a publican, ". . . the other side won't stand for it. And half of my trade comes from them." His brother John, a doctor, looks forward to advancement by association. Lily, his mother, sees in her son's experience, paradoxically, a kind of redemption for a certain slick self-esteem in his priestly office. But Father Carroll's release came because he signed a confession renouncing his faith. There had been no torture, no beatings. His apostasy was the climax to the less spectacular torment of five years' solitary confinement.

We learn this first from Tom Breslin, a local Trade Union organizer—"leading the young eejits of the town astray." The rest of the play takes up the consequences of the revelation, and particularly Father Carroll's own agonized inquisition of his motives. Communally, the hero-worship turns to hatred and an exercise in what Breslin sardonically calls "another dignified protest in the name of Holy Church. Another nail in Cromwell's coffin. . . . Let us now conclude our business by praying for the conversion of Russia." A priest calls to arrive at some exculpatory formula. He fails and the Bishop's visit is "postponed." John recalls petty dishonesties of his brother's youth, for which John regularly took the blame: "I think I must hate him! . . . You can't say John did it this time!"

Two people display understanding: Father Rooney, a "whiskey priest" who hears Carroll's confession; and his mother. Rooney, having given absolution, has now to deter Carroll from indulging a sense of guilt—"if you allow that seed to take root, you are unworthy to be a priest of God." Lily sees him, in his guilt and humiliation, "now more a priest than ever, because now you have His cross on you." He is to disappoint her again. As the play closes, he is shifting between broken memories of the prison and attempts to reconstruct the former Father Carroll—fashionable, influential, worldly.

As in the radio plays, the ending opens out on further
irresolution, not offering to solve anything.

The Blind Mice is open to criticism. In a sense it is
a "problem play," and it lines up too neatly the different atitudes to the problem—of good faith, conscience, charity. Tom Breslin, though an interesting
piece of social prophecy, seems to have strayed in from
some other play; and the mob's motive does not come
over with much conviction. Fundamentally, though, as
in all these plays, the shortcoming is linguistic. Friel
has said that dialogue is easy to write. But as he has
also said that a play exists essentially through its language, the dialogue that is easy to write has the precise
sense of the less intricate tracery of conversation between only two people. It is true that short stories
"function privately, man to man, a *personal* conversation. . . . But the dramatist functions through the
group; not a personal conversation but a public address" ("The Theatre of Hope and Despair"). The
language of *The Blind Mice* does not carry its situations and feelings. Perhaps at some distant level it is a
transmutation of Friel's own decision of conscience as
a novice at Maynooth. But it has not arrived at a form
of public address.

II

A writer, Friel once put it, always sings the same
song. In these early plays, which at the time he considered a self-indulgence, we hear only snatches of his
own. Motifs appear and vanish; themes elude full

articulation. Among them we may identify the faces and the masks of love and loyalty, the byways of family relationships, the commerce between individual and community life.

The Enemy Within was the first play to give these his melody. He calls it "a solid play. It's not good, but it was a commendable sort of a play. There's nothing very wrong with it and there's certainly nothing very good about it" (*Acorn*). With it he embarked upon what became a kind of tetralogy on the theme of love and family. Although *The Enemy Within* is set in the sixth century and Columba's Iona, Friel does not consider it, nor is it, a "historical play." Yet the withdrawal from the present time released him from the distractions of "contemporary relevance." The play sharply associates event and character with unintermitted theme.

As in most of the short stories, the setting is rural, whether in the island community, tending cattle, keeping the boats, stooking corn, or in Columba's memories of Ireland:

Out at the corn there, Cormac was cutting, and I was behind him, tying, and the sun was warm on my back, and I was stooped over, so that this bare, black exile was shrunk to a circle around my feet. And I was back in Tirconaill; and Cormac was Eoghan, my brother, humming to himself; and the dog that was barking was Ailbe, our sheep-dog; and there were trees at the bottom of the field as long as I did not look; and the blue sky was quick with larks as long as I did not lift my head; and the white point of Errigal mountain was behind my shoulder as long as I kept my eyes on the ground . . . and any minute my mother would come to the head of the hill

and strike the iron triangle to summon us in for food.
And when Cormac spoke I did not answer him because
I could not leave them, Caornan. As God is my judge,
I could not leave them.

The speech is not decorative lyricism, though lyrical
it is. It puts in words the persistent call of home for
Columba; and it translates from landscape the con-
flicts within him, which events bring to a head, between
the obligation to his family and that to his calling.

Hugh O'Neill, Columba's cousin, pleads with him
to come from Iona to bless their standards in battle,
the priest to abandon his "exile for God" to take sides
in worldly violence. His temptation is to the love of
family more than of God, to power and secular influence—the temptation, in many ways, of Eliot's
Beckett. Though torn, he agrees, against the admoni-
tion of his Prior, Grillaan.

By the time of Columba's return, his cousin vic-
torious, Caornan, the saintly copyist, has died, and
Columba must face a new temptation now, to atone by
a regimen harsh beyond due measure. Grillaan urges
him, "submit to the wise discipline of the monastery
and to it alone. . . . And beyond that—nothing." It
finally sustains Columba through continued trial: the
disappearance of Oswald, a young English novice whom
he has struck, fresh importunities from Ireland—"Family, Columb, family!" says his brother Eoghan, who,
his request refused, leaves Columba with his curses.
The end of the play is a beginning. Columba is one of
those whose path, as Grillaan had told him, demands

perpetually "the will and determination to begin, and then to begin again, and then to begin again, so that their whole life is a series of beginnings."

Friel here plainly enunciates a character, and a situation within the monastery that covers the relationships between the willful, energetic Columba and his various fellows, each of them seeing him in a different aspect. The structure of the play suggests a very deliberate act of composition, shaped as it is around the two major scenes, the appeals to Columba from his family, of which the crucial second one is markedly the longer. The design is craftsmanlike, if a little contrived. In contrast to its calculated neatness, there is often a fluidity of transition between scenes, an unforced growth of associations as in the sequence leading from Columba's distribution of gifts on his return from Ireland, through the report of Caornan's death, to Grillaan's account of his pastoral travels in Columba's absence. Columba thinks of his plans for Caornan, now never to be realized: "to release him from his exile and allow him to die in Ireland. A big room and a big table, and a small chair. They are waiting for him"; and Dochonna discloses Caornan's own wishes, to "go up to the Isles of Orkney and find a hermitage there . . . to do penance for all the joy he found in the life here." The sequence unobstrusively links the idea of exile, loss, home, and the endless quest of the spirit, in a manner that Friel was to develop in his later plays. The opening scenes, up to Columba's first reminiscences of home, preparing for the entry of Hugh's messenger, are emotionally low-keyed. They turn upon domestic routine and the humor of simple men. Columba and Grillaan retell a favorite old joke:

GRILLAAN: "Why are you working in the forge, Comgall?"
COLUMBA: "Because I was picked, Finnian."
GRILLAAN: "You're a Christian now, not a Pict! Get out!"

Then the deaf Domestic Manager, Dochonna, repeats the story, destroying the point. Monastery life, indeed, is seen realistically for what it must be, a good deal more of hard graft, humdrum duties, and horseplay of the novices, which offends Oswald, than the heights of spiritual crisis. The language, lively and idiomatic, confines itself to this level of experience:

GRILLAAN: The second calf was dead born; so I still have to see twin calves. The first one is quite sturdy though. And Brendan says with your permission he's going to call it Rufus.
COLUMBA: A red one, is it?
GRILLAAN: Black as a raven. Didn't you know? Brendan's colour-blind!
COLUMBA: He's not! Agh, someone should tell him! The novices will make a terrible fool of him!
GRILLAAN: Too late. They're finished in the cornfield, and they're all gathered round it, stroking it and admiring it, and saying it's the reddest calf they ever saw!. My goodness such a red calf! And Brendan's standing there as proud as if he were the father!

Beyond the community is the past of family and homeland. Columba is, as he says, "chained irrevocably to the earth, to the green wooded earth of Ireland," which is also "damned, damned, damned Ireland" and "a millstone round my neck." The sense of place is strong in his being. The play echoes with the names of his upbringing: Kilmacrenan, Carndonagh, Derry, Ballymagroarty, Coleraine, Aughnacloy.

These are the surroundings that evoke the recollections of both the beauty and the brutality that Columba, to become "a real exile," must deny: "the wrack of Gweebarra, the wood-pigeons in the oaks of Derry," and the headiness of battle:

> Ran like the hammers of Jericho down through Monaghahan and Cavan, and when we finally cornered them at a place called Cul-Fedha on the banks of the Blackwater, if they had half-a-dozen scamps behind them that was the height of it. And Sirinus, the monk—we had a good name for him—we called him the Brave Beetle because he was a wee black runt of a man and led the retreat as hard as he could go.

In another mood, its wastefulness stirs his compassion:

> I saw Colman Beg being split and fall from his horse. I ran to him as fast as I could although he was my enemy. But when I got to him he was dead, his white hair loose about the grass, his eyes open, his strong brown face calm and at peace.

Between this complex attachment and his calling, Columba must make his peace.

Looking back on the play, one might feel that it has more to do with Columba's relationship to Ireland—love, hatred, exile—than with a choice between that and the religious life. The play does not present the latter's claims with anything like the same power. Consequently, that side of Columba's conflict hardly becomes a credible adversary. When Ireland is a presence, feeling and the language that carries it pulse most strongly. They have different voices, all with a vernacular base, varying from the heightened lyric, frugally employed, to the coarser idiom of Eoghan and his son. To these, the "monastery scenes," which modulate to the more formal exchanges of the disputes between Columba and Grillaan, do add a further variant. From this mosaic of accents the play acquires its "public voice," functioning for the first time in the modes of drama. It is this, and its clearer apprehension of theme, that make the play a significant development.

3

Later Plays:
Themes and Variations

The Abbey Theatre's acceptance of *The Enemy Within* was Friel's first considerable recognition as a dramatist. The play's success encouraged productions of *The Blind Mice,* at the Eblana Theatre, Dublin; by the Northern Ireland BBC; then at the Lyric Theatre, Belfast. *The Enemy Within* was broadcast in a radio version in 1963, and nationally on BBC television in 1965—by which time Friel had written his first major play, *Philadelphia, Here I Come!*

The favorable reception of *The Enemy Within* did not distract Friel from the urgings of professional conscience. He was aware of a distance between himself and the innerness of dramatic experience, of too occasional an intimacy with theater electrically in action, and what goes to generate that excitement. To remedy this he arranged with Sir Tyrone Guthrie to spend five months of 1963 "hanging around"—his own term—the Tyrone Guthrie Theatre in Minneapolis, observing Guthrie at work as producer on *Hamlet* and *The Three Sisters*.

One result of the visit was the mortifying discovery that "the few plays I had written . . . were, in sad truth, tedious, tendentious and terribly boring." More positively it coalesced and quickened the scattered perceptions of theatrical means and ends, beyond just a knowledge of conventions and techniques. The whole theatrical experience, the "strange ritual of make-believe," came alive. Friel learned, he says,

> in Guthrie's own words, that theatre is an attempt to create something which will, if only for a brief moment, transport a few fellow travellers on our strange, amusing, perilous journey—a lift, but not, I hope, an uplift. I learned that the playwright's first function is to entertain, to have audiences enjoy themselves, to move them emotionally, to make them laugh and cry and gasp and hold their breath and sit on the edge of their seats and—again to quote the great man himself—"to participate in lavish and luxurious goings-on!"

From this illumination came *Philadelphia,* of a totally different order of achievement from its predecessors.

The play is divided into three "Episodes," the last of them in two parts. Its action occupies about eight hours of the evening before Gareth O'Donnell, sponsored by an aunt, is to leave Donegal, his widowed father, and their run-down general shop, for a hotel job in America. Each Episode specifically marks the hour, a suggestion of strictly chronological progression that frames the fluent dissolves between present time and the past that composed it. In a sense there is no progression. We leave Gar as we found him, about to emigrate and tormented by his decision. The play makes up the answer to his final question, "why do you have to leave? Why? Why?"

One can understand Friel's mild exasperation with audience misapprehensions, which include the backstage query, "Did young Gareth O'Donnell really emigrate from the old country"; a matronly explosion, "So he's coming to Philadelphia! So what the hell's he crying about!"; and the ingenious, "Mark my words, Harmon: the housekeeper's the father's mistress, and Gareth is their ill-egitimate son, and *he's* having an affair with the doctor's wife. My goodness, real shanty Irish!" The logic of the play is not in plot contrivance or "what-happens-next," but in its delicate montage of past and present experience and feeling.

Technically, the most striking device is the representation of Gar by two actors, one the Public, the other the Private, self. Through them, we see him, within the present of this life with father, relive his crucial memories. To his father (S. B. O'Donnell, "Screwballs" to his son), the Public Gar is taciturn, sullen, resenting the social and emotional deadends of Ballybeg, largely epitomized for him by his father. Other relationships disclose the sensibility he is thus at pains to conceal. With Madge, the old housekeeper, he is confiding, at ease. In the opening scenes he is exuberant, in a mood of release, to an extent feigned, a sort of whistling in the dark, but still betokening a natural generosity of spirit. In this disposition, complicating qualities and attitudes take their place.

The Private Gar—unseen by the other actors, "heard" on stage only by his alter ego—voices thoughts and feelings publicly unuttered, the ceaseless interior life which in actuality never formulates itself in words, even in the mind. The relationship between the two Gars is involved. Through all their variety of moods, Public and Private are convincingly a single person, sharing, for example, both their sardonic, surrealistic humour, and their vulnerable affections. The Private Gar, at times amenable to the Public's role-playing, ready on occasion to divert his misgivings, will at other times, turning Public's defenses, force into the open feelings of which the composite Gar fights shy. The deeper searchings come only gradually. The audience is first engrossed in Gar's situation through brilliantly comic exchanges. Developing the tone of Public's euphoria, they make an aggressively paced opening to Episode I, and set off the contrasts to come.

Much of what defines Gar takes place in Episode I. Madge, a spinster, represents something of the life he is leaving, devoted without much return of gratitude to her sister's family and their children. Chance recalls Gar's mother to him, dead three days after his birth, a peasant girl, and by Madge's report, "wild and young," the antithesis of his father. The schoolmaster calls, once a suitor of Gar's mother, now a seedy mountebank, but among the few to acknowledge Gar's departure. Like S. B., he is one of Gar's possible futures.

O'Donnell senior has given no sign of the day's

being a special occasion. "At six o'clock," Gar tells
Madge, "he remembered about the bloody pollock,
and him in the middle of the Angelus [*stands in imita-
tion of the Father: head bowed, hands on chest. In
flat tones—*] Behold-the-handmaid-of-the-Lord-Gut-and-
salt-them-fish." Public and Private anticipate and
parody his costive social and conversational rituals
when, false teeth on the tea table, he doles out his
banalities—"I didn't find as many [rats] about the year."
"That old rapier wit,'" Private comments over the
silence, but he longs too for their feelings to meet, for
"one unpredictable remark," one shared expressive
memory. His speech of unspoken wishes dies on his
father's repeated, "I didn't find as many about the
year," deflationary comic in force, but affectingly sum-
ming up the distance between them.

Many such particular contrasts typify the general
pattern of shifting moods. Private's suggested "unpredictable remarks" vary from "I like to walk across the
White Strand when there's a misty rain falling" to the
coarse "stick it out here with me for it's not such a
bad aul' bugger of a place." The dialogues of Public
and Private range between their requiem for the dead
mother and conceits of Gar as a celebrated footballer
or musician ("O'Donnell's simultaneous wielding of
baton and bow is the greatest thing since Leather Ass
died.") Then out of the buffoonery comes the elegiac
memory of the mother. The two Gars ape a series of
Hollywood-American stereotypes (cowboy, ambitious
immigrant and employer) and, as fashion-show *com-
père*, Private guys S.B.'s preparations for tea:

The pert little apron is detachable—[*S. B. removes apron*] —thank you, Marie Celeste—and underneath we have the tapered Italian-line slacks in ocelot. I would draw your attention to the large collar stud. . . . We call this seductive outfit 'Indiscretion'. It can be worn six days a week, in or out of bed. [*In polite tone.*] Have a seat Screwballs. [*S. B. sits down at table.*] Thank you. Remove the hat. [*S. B. takes off the hat to say grace.*]

and so on into the deadly familiar conversation. Toward his father Gar has not a resolved attitude, but incessantly fluctuating responses. He despises, loves, tolerates, disregards S.B. On only one occasion, and even that is doubtful, did their individual tunes, as Friel has put it, strike the same key and so make possible a harmony.

The father/son relationship dominates Episode I. Within it, and central in the Episode, comes the re-enactment, urged by Private on a reluctant Public, of the evening when, tongue-tied by nervousness, Gar surrenders his sweetheart, Kate Doogan, to her father's notion of a better marriage prospect. The "present" of bedroom and kitchen fades, leaving empty space to the young lovers. To Private's astringent commentary —"a sore hoke on the aul' prestige . . . a deep scar on the aul' skitter of a soul, eh?"—and inept rehearsal of the meeting with Senator Doogan, Gar retreats demoralized from his buoyant proposals of marriage, home, and family—"very well preserved for a father of 14 children," Private says later.

It is a scene—young love, love despised, naivety self-betrayed—that could be easily sentimentalized. Foregoing his rhetorical skills, Friel achieves tenderness by

Gar's less articulate candor and striving after dignity (his ludicrous "egg-money" profits) . The interchanges of the scene itself, as much as Private's caustic depreciation of it, secure its poignancy against mawkishness. The same is true of the encounter with Boyle, intensely moving, but devoid of any directly emotional language. The following sequence, which follows Boyle's incidental revelations of his failure, reaches into emotions not even alluded to by the words:

BOYLE: Good luck, Gareth.
PUBLIC: Thanks, Master.
BOYLE: Forget Ballybeg and Ireland.
PUBLIC: It's easier said.
BOYLE: Perhaps you'll write me.
PUBLIC: I will indeed.
BOYLE: Yes, the first year. Maybe the second. I'll—I'll miss you, Gar.
PRIVATE: For God's sake get a grip on yourself.
PUBLIC: Thanks for the book and for—
    [*Boyle embraces Public briefly.*]
PRIVATE: Stop it! Stop it! Stop it!

It leaves Gar at the end of the Episode almost responseless to Private's remonstration, "Don't be a damned sentimental fool!"

Episode II intensifies Gar's effort to cast off "memories and images and impressions that are going to make you bloody miserable." Private is less intrusive, less vocal, the cross talk of the two Gars less often funny. After the opening fireworks a different tension builds, the pressure tighter, feelings near breaking point. It communicates itself to Madge. She snaps capriciously at S.B., who, in his forlorn gaze at Gar's

bedroom, manifests the desolation he has no words
for.

Different aspects of the present and another possible
future press their claims. Gar is waiting for "the boys"
to come and say goodbye. When they do, they open another of Ballybeg's confined perspectives. Their endless
reminiscence of imaginary seductions conceals a reality
of futile street wanderings, of cold, of locked doors,
and of drawn blinds. But their fragile camaraderie, with
its cadences of silence, embarrassed by Gar's leave-tak-
ing, calls on Gar's uncertain loyalties with something
that memory may "distil of all its coarseness." The
future of the reenacted visit by his childless, tippling,
Irish-American aunt arouses, in Private, dread of an
oppressive motherliness as claustrophobic as anything
in Ballybeg.

All the vistas forebode blind alleys, culminating in
Kate Doogan's farewell visit. It elicits from Gar a
reprise of the accumulated memories and motifs, the
entreaties of home still unsuppressed. Their origin may
be in the past, in "a great happiness" shared between
son and father "fishing on a lake on a showery day."
But Gar can draw no memory of it from S.B. His attempts thread amongst S.B.'s regular chess game with
the local Canon, hilariously amusing as Private im-
provises on their hoary pleasantries, and bitterly satirical of the Canon's smug incomprehension. In the dead
early hours, the remembered open prospects of the past
recede; may, indeed, never have been.

Philadelphia delighted most of the reviewers, though
it sometimes left them unsure on their feet. It travesties

the play to ascribe to it "a sweet atmosphere of resigna-
tion." Private does much more than laugh when the
hero cries and cry when he laughs. One critic, com-
plaining of prosaic dialogue, absurdly cited one of the
Canon's platitudes as being "about as lyrical as Friel
ever gets." In fact, some of the scenes run the opposite
risk, of verbal overload, of becoming a series of ora-
torical "turns." Friel, however, is suspicious of the Irish
facility with an assortment of Synge-songs, sceptical, for
instance, of such a received triumph as O'Casey's "Take
away their hearts of stone. . . ." His lyricism is sparing,
but, when the scene demands, responsive:

> PRIVATE [. . . *thrusts his face between the players.*] D'you
> hear it? D'you know what the music says? [*To
> S. B.*] It says that once upon a time a boy and
> his father sat in a blue boat on a lake on an
> afternoon in May, and on that afternoon a great
> beauty happened, a beauty that has haunted the
> boy ever since, because he wonders now did it
> really take place or did he imagine it? There
> are only the two of us, he says; each of us is
> all the other has; and why can we not even
> look at each other?

Pieces like this do not function in isolation. They
work with all the varieties of rhetoric to give the play
its shape and the characters their substance. Gar's part
dominates but does not drown out the others. S.B. too
would have his Private voice. The situation and its
people exist in depth, through Friel's discerning man-
agement of the kinds of statement made accessible by
Joyce and O'Neill; and to an extent, though Friel

would disagree, by Beckett, if one can conceive of
Beckett without the grotesque.

It is a statement first of all, and necessarily, about
particular people in a particular grouping. More generally, it is a statement about Ireland, the Ireland of
religious and sexual frigidity, of overbearing old age,
of joyless, close-mouthed rural puritanism; and of their
opposites. The play's humor reflects them and is often,
understandably, savage enough. Gar likes Madge; she
is also, callously, "aul' fluke-feet."

Beyond these peculiarly regional truths, its ironies
and an underlayer of certain images carry the play to
a wider statement still. Gar's—especially Private's—
eloquence, and the inarticulateness it operates on and
variously responds to, set up a pattern of speech and
silence that enlarges the personal failures of communi-
cation. Ample scenes, notably in Gar's symbolic recol-
lection, accentuate the restrictions of closed-up doors
and streets, material images of their spiritual counterparts. Ultimately, the play is talking in the broadest
terms about estrangement, loneliness, and human hopes
of understanding and intimacy. Unequivocally "Irish,"
Philadelphia traverses its regional boundaries.

The language of *The Loves of Cass McGuire,* like
that of *Philadelphia,* is naturalistic. Raised and tensed
above its actual speech models, it is perfectly authentic
in all its registers, remarkably so in Cass's own Ameri-
canized idiom. Again, too, it is the language that carries the transitions of mood and, especially here, of
perception. For *Cass,* like some of the short stories, is
about escape, and the accelerating process of escape,

from reality to dreams, an impairment of vision willed or accepted.

The situation so formulated is the commonplace of the immigrant returned. Having left Ireland at eighteen, Cass has come back after fifty-two years in America, a life on the edge of Skid Row and well beneath respectability, to a family, as she says, "not too sure if she's a maiden aunt at all." Her mother, now senile, has forgotten her. Harry McGuire, her brother, and his wife, Alice, pack her off from their own house to an old people's home when her rowdiness and drinking become a scandal. She is, she learns to her dismay, self-sufficient; the money she had painfully sent home over the years has, unneeded, been kept for her. In the home, her hardy attachment to life and the present breaks down. Emulating two of the inmates, Trilbe Costello and Mr. Ingram, she edits her past into fantasy, which displaces intolerable fact.

Make-believe, of various degrees of consequence, is pervasive. Tessa, the maid at Eden House, is engaged to an apprentice bricklayer, of whom she likes to talk, without too much conviction, as a building contractor. Dom, the McGuire son, cultivates adolescent worlds of pulp-magazine crime. The grandmother, with self-possessed battiness, enacts her faraway scenes remote from what is around her. Harry's children, like the children of the radio plays, have grown away from the family; in Alice's romancings to Cass, they still attend the Christmas gathering, all their failings censored in her mind.

Cass is at first a gust of vulgar scepticism in

this prudish gentility. She knew Alice's father, "who couldn't keep his hands off young girls." She drinks, and brawls in a local pub. She draws liberally on her fund of dirty jokes and ribald speech, increasingly so as Harry's plan to "make up for all the lost years" comes down to occasional visits to what Cass persists in calling the workhouse. Cass's huge vitality and gutter eloquence—"I pulled the chain on better-looking things," she quotes an American friend on herself— appear strong enough to shatter the empty refinement of the McGuires. "Well," she says with satisfaction, "that stirred things up a bit, dinnit?"

Though it draws spiritedly on the convention, the play is not a comedy of manners. That serves rather the purpose T. S. Eliot saw in the "meaning" of a poem, to distract the reader while the poem does its real work. Here, to begin with, the chronology is disturbed, and disturbing. Cass's auspicious welcome home does not take place until Act II. The play apparently opens in the McGuires' living-room on the morning after Cass's spree at the pub.

On her entrance, Cass quarrels with Harry, talking directly to the audience, about where the play should begin:

> The story begins where I say it begins, and I say it begins with me stuck in the gawddam workhouse! So you can all get the hell outa here!

The scene becomes her bedroom there. She confides some of her past to the audience, resists an attempt by

Harry to recall memories of her father, then moves out to what is now the Eden House common room and to the other residents. The stage briefly returns to the McGuires', as Harry tells her she must leave. The final sequence, back in Eden House, is with Ingram and Trilbe, for whom the audience Cass again addresses is nonexistent.

Thereafter, apart from the homecoming of Act II, the scene remains stable at Eden House, increasingly invaded by Cass's memories, regrets, desolation. As throughout Act I, she resists, more and more despairingly, the fading of the present: "I don't go in for the fond memory racket!" "I don't want to remember."

> I live in the present . . . if things get too rough I can go and hide in the signal box. I've always got places I can go to . . . always . . . you bet . . . a dozen of them . . . out to the crooked bridge . . . at the back of the mill. . . . But the signal box . . . it's the safest . . . no one ever looks there. . . . Where are you? Jeeze, where are you?

Her appeal is to the audience. By the time she wakens in Act III, she has retreated from the world they represent: "Where the hell is everyone? . . . I could ov swore there were folks out there." The new arrival, Miss Butcher, her self-confidence not yet broken, continues to address them: "Lunatics is sane compared with these ones!" Cass, like Ingram, Trilbe, and inevitably Miss Butcher, will invite the solace of a reconstructed past:

And we moved into this great ten-roomed apartment on the West side, and from our bedroom window we could see the ships sailing off to South America and the Bahamas . . . and Ireland . . . and Glasgow. . . . And all around the walls were pictures of Harry's kids; I was their Auntie Cass, you see; and regular as the clock came their letters—I have them all—fine kids.

There is an absorbing dramatic tension between the play's apparent promise of social comedy, and the gradual dissolution of Cass's will, where the real conflict is taking place. The transactions with the audience evolve into a dynamic emblem of the diminishing contact that Cass is striving to preserve, nicely pointed by the late introduction of Miss Butcher. The fluidity of time and setting, equally functional, corresponds to Cass's own vacillations, as past and present threaten to coalesce into dream. It protracts, as well, the sense of the term of Cass's decline. This occupies two weeks of "actual" time, foreshortened because it is represented on stage by the events of only a morning, an afternoon, and an evening. The "rhapsodies," as Friel calls them, by suspending the normal passage of time, also allow for the wasting of Cass's resolution, and in a number of ways act as a kind of dramatic shorthand.

In Friel's words, "Each of the three characters who rhapsodize—Trilbe, Ingram and Cass—takes the shabby and unpromising threads of his past life and weaves it into a hymn of joy, a gay and rapturous and exaggerated celebration of a beauty that might have been." Ingram and Trilbe initiate them, one in each act. Trilbe's own, toward the close of Act I, is typical.

Slowly she builds up a myth of enchanted years of love and wandering, the heightened, echoing language withdrawing her into a sphere of her own:

TRILBE: Travelling, moving, visiting strange places, meeting new people, with Gordon beside me.

INGRAM: My little golden Trilbe.

TRILBE: And the servants and the music and the wine and the travel and the poetry and his love for me and my love for him . . . all so real. My Gordon from Arles on the Loire, my prince from Edinburgh in Provence . . . my father resting in the afternoon, my journeys to the Nile and the Volga, the road to Samarkand, the road, the traveller's road . . .

INGRAM: Trilbe.

TRILBE: Gordon McClelland.

INGRAM: Golden Trilbe.

TRILBE: My highland prince.

INGRAM: My little golden Trilbe.

TRILBE: Say it slowly after me: *But I, being poor, have only my dreams.*

INGRAM: Our truth.

TRILBE: *I have spread my dreams under your feet./ Tread softly because you tread on my dreams.*

INGRAM: Our truth.

Of these fabrications, her own life, as an amateurish elocution teacher with a drunken father, is a travesty. So in Act II is Ingram's of his, and Cass's in Act III.

The diction is totally at odds with Cass's vernacular coarseness and the McGuires' affectations. Surmounting the difficult problem of being true both to Trilbe's novelettish fancy and an experience much more intense, it makes heavy demands on the actors. Naturalistically, and for most of the action, Trilbe has an un-

conscious zaniness and a madly cultivated articulation.
Her opening scene with Ingram in Act III, superbly
inconsequential, darts round news items ("The tem-
perature in Sydney yesterday was 97 degrees"), problematical reminiscence (her brother "was a diver—a
diver—a diver. And a professional diver—just dives,
doesn't he?"), and the doings of the home:

TESSA:	Matron says would youse rather a concert or a fillim tomorrow night?
INGRAM:	I . . . I really don't . . .
TRILBE:	A concert or a film; let us analyse this. Who would be the artists in the concert?
TESSA:	How would I know? The fillim is called—
TRILBE:	Film, child, film. One syllable. Film.
TESSA:	*General Custer's Last Stand.*
TRILBE:	That sounds familiar. (To Ingram) Who was General Custer?
INGRAM:	Wasn't he one of the leaders of your Easter Rebellion?
TRILBE:	I do believe you're right. (To Tessa) Yes, I vote for the film.

The rhapsodies must take on an entirely unnaturalis-
tic inflection. Their intention is not to represent literally any real form of neurotic behavior. They are
stylized expressions, dramatic allegories, of a psychological state that compensates for painful fact in the
refuge of a private world. Physically, the rhapsodists
are isolated by the placing of the armchair, otherwise
unused, which each of them occupies in turn: an
"otherness" of time and place that condenses the course
of Cass's decline.

These ritual excursions come off as a dramatic contrivance because the body of the play so firmly estab-
lishes, in realistic terms, the bewildered suffering of
the participants. Certain quite brief, unembellished
scenes convey the authentic human essence. The jaunty
departure of Pat Quinn, the only resident to get away
from Eden House, impresses on the others their continuing exile from companionship, Cass in total silence,
Trilbe and Ingram in a rattle of disjointed conversation
that dies on them. When Cass learns how futile were
her gifts of money, she registers the impact soundlessly
and in broken questions. Another of her loves has gone
the way of the rest, all of them abortive or without
dignity, with only a few moments of tenderness in a
drab, low-life procession.

Cass's last line, as she looks round the common room
is: "Home at last. Gee, but it's a good thing to be
home." Though Cass has concluded a kind of armistice,
a release of sorts for her, hers is for the audience a
pitiable end. The theme of the concerto in which she
is soloist is not the "bittersweet" one that, as a reviewer
saw it, home is, comfortingly, where you have your
dreams. Cass is not Mother Machree. The proposition
is the bleaker one that human beings can endure only
so much before some psychological escape mechanism
operates, however wastefully, to bring relief. The sense
of the play is of loss, waste, defeat, neither cosy nor
consoling.

The nucleus of Cass may lie in Aunt Lizzy of *Philadelphia,* combined with one potential outcome of Gar's
American expectations. Cass is, as Gar might be, a

"failed" Aunt Lizzy, ending up like James Madden in Brian Moore's *Judith Hearne*. This is, of course, speculative biography, without much bearing on the plays as they exist. It does, however, argue for Friel's continuing exploration of related themes, whose application, while localized, is not restricted by their Irish setting. He looks on these two plays, together with *Lovers* and *Crystal and Fox,* as inspections of the diversities of love, undertaken in the way that a sculptor views his work from different angles. From this point of view, Part I of *Lovers* might originate from a latent sequence in the lives of Gar and Kate, Joe Brennan and Mag Enright being their proxies. Mag is pregnant; they are to be married in three weeks.

"Winners" appears on the face of it a much less complex venture than either *Philadelphia* or *Cass.* Only one relationship, that of Mag and Joe, is directly presented. The only special device is to employ two commentators (or one) on the action. They fill in the family and social background. From them we gradually learn, as a descant to the idyllic morning spent by the two young lovers on the hill outside Ballymore, that its sequel is their death by drowning. Whether by accident or suicide is left open and is, according to Friel, irrelevant.

The narrators' tone is "impersonal, completely without emotion. . . . At no time must they reveal an attitude to their material." Most of their prose, in the flat periods of an official report, is in keeping with this disinterestedness:

Joseph Brennan was the only child of Mick and Nora Brennan. Because of his asthma, Mick Brennan has not had a job for over twenty years. He receives unemployment benefit and this is supplemented by the earnings of his wife, who works as a charwoman from 8:00 a.m. until 8:00 p.m., six days a week, for 2/6 an hour.

Only once do they seem to testify to an emotional leaning:

. . . . We can assume that they talked some and perhaps dreamed some, because they were young and the day was beautiful.

For the rest they are a detached Chorus, matter-of-factly concluding that after the event, "Life there goes on as usual. As if nothing had ever happened."

Among these interventions, Joe and Mag banter, quarrel, make their peace, poke fun at their elders: the nuns; the Fathers; their landlord-to-be, a gruesomely enthusiastic abattoir owner. In the course of this, while their charm augments the deadpan reporting, they intimate in their present laughter its future hazards. Madge's erratic efforts to study, a minor friction, provoke Joe's ambition to the age-old male complaint: "You trapped me into marrying you—that's all right—I'll marry you . . . somehow—somehow I'll get a degree and be a maths teacher. And nobody, neither you nor your precious baby nor anyone else, is going to stop me!" Madge's weeping clouds their earlier good humor, even about the nasty flat above the slaughterhouse yard.

It is Joe who slowly reconciles them, as he does in the corresponding bitterness of Episode II, which arises from their social disparity. Mag's family is well-to-do, her father a dentist. Joe has turned down offers to live with them, to decorate the flat, and takes offense at a snide remark of Mag's about his parents. He moves from injured dignity to clowning. They wrestle, kiss, and as they leave the hill:

MAG: Come on, Joe! Let's begin the future now!
JOE: You're nuts.

Underlying that future is the web of implications they have unwittingly divulged. In less resilient years, the slaughterhouse will be less a joke, the hoped-for degree less an exhilaration, or, if abandoned—as Joe magnanimously proposes—a spur to the resentment over unplanned parenthood and marriage.

A more amiable future is of course surmisable. Most of the insinuation appears to be against it. The engaging generosity that now gets the better of disgruntlement is at risk. Joe and Mag are winners because death forestalls a corruption of love: "Forever wilt thou love and she be fair." All the adult lives we hear of (including the marriage in Part II, "Losers") are blemished: Mrs. Brennan's drudgery, the loss of Joe, "all her dreams and love and hope and delight"; Mick Brennan, as Joe tells us, hoarding his son's school reports, then, after the funeral, burning them; Mr. Enright's failing practice, aimless nights; his wife's engrained psychotic despair, spending her bad days in bed wearing dark glasses; the death of Mag's twin brother in infancy followed by the death of Mag herself. The play admits such an interpretation and is clearly calling on a much more complex set of references than just the young couple in isolation.

They are part of a community, even its physical detail discreetly glimpsed through their conversation. The Commentators—"omniscient" beyond the style of report they affect—mediate the mobile emotions of Joe and Mag's conversation. Both, in turn, are inset with the usages of other lives. All together they make up a tissue of ironies whose relevance to "Losers" may not be at once apparent.

"Winners" and "Losers" are presented as a single play, though they share neither characters nor story. Joe and Mag are youths in love, unaffectedly eloquent, romantic ("Propose to me," Mag insists to Joe). The couple in "Losers," though they court with fire enough, are in the shorter-winded love of middle age. Andy Traynor (the Andy of "The Highwayman and the Saint") makes no more ardent declaration than, "You're looking nice, Hanna." He is the narrator, chatting to the audience, which is sitting in, so to speak, in place of a confidant. The events unfolded by his account and the enacted scenes are those of the short story.

The only additional character in the play is "prissy Cissy" Cassidy, Mrs. Wilson's familiar. She is a phrasebook of worshipful cliché ("Thanks be to God," all her cry for the daily round), "sickly piousity," and a readily disgusted suspicion of men. Andy's drunk scene satisfies her prim aversions. Through his denunciation of St. Philomena runs her litany of principle now confirmed: "All men is animals—brute animals. . . . Brutes of the field." Cissy, however, falls far short of Mrs. Wilson's stratagems of hypochondriac martyrdom ("A wee bit of discomfort's good for me"), erudite devotions ("Saint Hyacintha de Mariscottis, look after us this day and this night."), and relentless self-posses-sion ("Don't worry. I'll settle him. And stop whing-ing!").

The combination worsts Andy, who has only the one brief victory. He accepts his lot fatalistically ("You've got to admire the aul' bitch. She could handle a regiment"), defeated but not finally tamed. His com-mentary retains a residue of his old scepticism:

> And a funny thing about that bloody bell, too. You know, before, if there was no noise coming from down-stairs, the ringing would be enough to waken the dead. But *after* we got married, it only went when Hanna and me started talking. Wasn't that perverse now, eh? Oh, a deep one; deep as a well.

His subjection is less total than in the short story, because after the catastrophe he voices thoughts to which it gives no place. He is fully aware of what has happened: "But, like, to see a woman that had plenty of spark in her at one time and then to see her turn before your very eyes into a younger image of her mother, by God it's strange, I'll tell you, very peculiar."

The sentiment echoes "Winners," where Joe reflects on the adaptations of family life: "That's the way married people go. They even begin to look alike.

Wonder is old Skinny Skeehan married? I bet she looks like a gatepost." One way or another, marriage and family erode individualism. Mag feels that she and Joe will "never become like that, because—don't laugh at me, Joe—because I think we're unique." Andy and Hanna would come in the category she describes, who don't know "what being in love really is." From these destinies, Joe and Mag feel set apart, even though Joe does say of Mag's father, "I'd like to be like him. God, such a fine man."

These resonances between the plays enlighten their joint meaning. There is perhaps a virtue in the adult lives: in Andy's sardonic self-containment; in Mrs. Enright's endurance, her "health improved. She has not had a relapse for almost seven months"; in the sympathy of Nora Brennan, who visits Mrs. Enright in hospital. The plays remark in the lives of their characters not only that death in a sense makes winners of Joe and Mag. They say as well that human beings, put to it, may make the best of however bad a bargain. The ironies are multiple, not at all a simple favoring of Joe and Mag over Andy and Hanna, easeful death over nagging life. It is a view not consoling and certainly not sentimentalized.

Lovers scrutinizes some of the components—romantic, Christian, practical—informing the popular concept of love, which encourages expectations that reality is unlikely to gratify. There may, however, on the stage, be some imbalance in its parts that distorts the refinements of what it says. In "Losers," though Andy's colloquies are in a ruminative minor key, the comedy is

robust, broadly satirical, drawing on farce in the love
scenes and the drunk scene. These pay off handsomely
in laughs, but in spite of the downbeat conclusion,
tend to muffle the echoes, which need to be heard,
from the more lyrical pitch of "Winners." The primary
contrast between the two pieces is apt to assert itself
over the finer distinctions of meaning. There is a
particular temptation for actors to overplay for the
laughs, which will blur the close integrity of the two
parts, and their structural purposefulness.

"Happiness," Swift said, "is a perpetual possession
of being well deceived." The protagonists of *Lovers,*
like Gar and Cass, test the proposition in the fertile
ground of love and family, one conclusion being that
the deception is not always easily achieved or main-
tained. Technically, *Lovers* contrives to establish, by
allusion, from a much smaller number of characters,
the same range of relationships directly presented in
Philadelphia and *Cass.* In all three plays the families
are bourgeois, rooted, indeed stagnating, in the narrow
certainties of small-town life. *Crystal and Fox* turns to
the fringe society of traveling people.

Despite the difference of setting, *Crystal and Fox*
is in the sequence of its predecessors. In Friel's development, however, its correspondences with *The Gentle
Island* are more interesting. In between these two came
The Mundy Scheme, a play of a kind he does not intend
to attempt again, so unlike all his others that it calls
for separate consideration.

The Mundy Scheme first came to notice when the
Abbey Theatre, following its ungenerous precedents,

turned it down. Its premise is Ireland as the *petit-bourgeois* Republic on which W. B. Yeats, with the pleasure of self-fulfilling alarms, fed his Anglo-Irish disdain. In the play, Homer Mundy, at a time of financial crisis, comes to the aid of the Irish government with a lucrative plan to turn most of the west of Ireland into an international cemetery.

He thus supplies the Prime Minister (F. X. Ryan) with a marketable alternative ("Irish Christianity once more leads the world in ecumenism and charity") to Pentagon overtures for nuclear bases in Cork and Galway (". . . you couldn't begin to give away our exports in Europe"). A rump Cabinet's agreement opens the scheme to the venal and rapidly double-crossing conspiracies of the Prime Minister and (involuntarily) selected colleagues. The end, with the scheme launched, leaves Ryan and his External Affairs Minister, Michael Moloney, in distrustful alliance.

Almost no folly is too witless for a government somewhere not to have at least entertained the idea of it. *The Mundy Scheme* does no great violence to the banes of Irish polity—witness the "Donegal Mafia," "family seats" in the Dáil, the burlesque proceedings of the Arms and other trials—which attained their amplest flower in the American export version. Too often the Republic is the North's not-so-secret weapon. This is the unlovely ambiance of *The Mundy Scheme*.

The first act picks off with scathing accuracy its peculiar mixture of *faux-bonhomie*, roguery, and professional chauvinism. In the credible predicament of national insolvency, Ryan is in search of what would

pass for an honorable solution, that is, good for the
Party, galling to the Opposition, and if possible not
harmful to the country. The quandary musters his
entire repertoire of poses, between which and natural
feelings he can no longer distinguish. His colleagues
personify the Irish political gallery of faithful hacks
and local celebrities rewarded. Moloney, with the bag-
man's foot-in-the-door come-ons, finally spells out the
providential scheme.

A delirious "Cabinet meeting" carries the first part
of Act II. During it, the participants contrive to camou-
flage the scheme's real nature from themselves under
a bureaucratic veil. The details have an insane plausibility.

BOYLE: Is the—are the—the—?
MOLONEY: Let's call it freight.
BOYLE: Is it subject to import duty?
MOLONEY: I'll have to get a ruling on that, Neil.
              Had the freight come unpacked, it would
              certainly be subject to import duty. But since
              it arrives packaged and sealed in containers
              previously manufactured in this country, un-
              der Section 73a of the 1933 Act, it may be
              deemed to be a reimported export—and con-
              sequently not subject to duty.
BOYLE: A big loss.
MOLONEY: We'll make up for it with the containers,
              which are shipped out on the empty planes.

The act ends in a flurry of land-piracy, eavesdropping,
and joint chicanery. This really marks the apex of the
play's development. In Act III plot and counterplot
run their devious courses. The cunning win through,

the less cunning go down, the dupes remain in ig-
norance. After the inauguration and a rambling Min-
isterial carouse, Ireland is left with the Mundy scheme.

The observation of manners in the final act is as
acute as ever, but invention has somehow flagged. It
is difficult to explain this relaxation. In conception,
Mundy has aims beyond a mere *jeu d'esprit,* and in
the greater part of its execution fulfills its aims. The
scheme itself isolates perfectly just those sore spots
which Friel wants to interrogate: shoneenism, xeno-
phobia, time-serving religion, even the Irish death-wish
—characteristics that invert the stereotype of tourist
brochures.

Perhaps the immediate vehicle of the satire is too
absurd. Its metaphorical felicity is not brought finally
into line with the serious satirical purposes. Though
the characters are externally observed public "hu-
mours" (not much comes of Ryan's relationship with
his mother, to which the stage directions give some
prominence), their attitudes have nearer counterparts
in life than the project that exercises them. *Mundy*
makes its admirable points with considerable and en-
tertaining verve, but leaves the feeling that there are
larger objectives potential in it.

Mundy's characters have the kind of reality appropriate to satire. Without the psychological depth of
the other plays, they exist as creatures of a strictly
limited situation, designed to lampoon types of political
behavior. The characters' private faces are entirely a
part of their public places. *Crystal and Fox* too is about
public maskers, Fox Melarkey and his wife Crystal,

entertainers, proprietors of a traveling show on its last
legs. Here there is a private life at much more complex
variance with professional role.

These traveling shows still tour the Irish villages,
though nowadays rarely incorporating, as Melarkey's
does, a play. From what we see of it, this one, *The
Doctor's Story,* is evidently a very bad play, not en-
hanced by its presentation. It is a sentimental drama
of the mission field and love. Crystal is the Mother
Superior. The show's conjurer and his wife, El Cid
and Tanya, are the young lovers. There is some shaky
French for atmosphere, and the dialogue painstakingly
reports the narrative line. Fox regards it and its audience—"All the hoors want is a happy ending"—with
total contempt.

This audience, unseen, occasionally audible off-stage,
hears the Fox of the showman's patter—mildly vulgar
stories, repartee, chat, and wheedle. To Crystal he
adopts the actor's patois—"My sweet," "My queen,"
"Exquisite, my love." Offensively heedless of El Cid's
pretensions, he makes no effort to dissuade him from
taking up with a rival company. Why, he cannot say.
"If I knew a simple answer to that," he tells Crystal,
"I'd go in for telling fortunes."

Pedro, devoted to the performing dog that is his
contribution to the bill, describes Fox as he was:

> Eight—ten years ago—my God he was on top of his form
> then! Cracking jokes, striding about, giving orders like
> a king; and everywhere he went Gabby [his son] perched
> up there on top of his shoulders. . . . Not a showman in
> the country to touch him!

The surface of his assurance remains in Fox's dealings. Hearing him, one might almost forget his theatre's broken seats, holey roof, and the run-down truck. His poise, however, is infirm. Under it are weariness and bafflement, declared by seeming incidentals of behavior still largely in control.

These appear in his dreamy isolation in his quarrel with El Cid: to Crystal's pleas he returns only aimless questions or bland agreement. After this setback he returns to Crystal and Pedro singing, full of bounce, then bitterly challenging all their lives together, "Round and round in circles. Same conversations, same jokes, same yahoo audiences; just like your Gringo, Pedro, eh?—doing the same old tricks again and again, and all you want is a little cube of sugar as a reward." El Cid, with some perception, has said that Fox will go on "until he's ratted on everybody." Crystal, thinking of times when things have promised better, recalls how Fox "makes trouble . . . he goes all sort of quiet."

Throughout the first act the portents increasingly assert themselves, most baleful in conversation with Pedro. Fox wonders if, at a moment of sudden moonlight, Gringo might not prefer to "all the sugar cubes in the world just one little saucer of arsenic"; and if he did, whether Pedro would love him enough to supply it. The menace, an undergrowth of violence, persists through Fox's memory of his meeting Crystal. The silent arrival of a motorcycle policeman in all his gear physically embodies it, as he warns them to move on the next morning. It moves closer to the foreground with the return of Gabriel (Gabby), on the run for, as it turns out, attempted manslaughter, though it might have been murder: "So I hit her again. And again . . . ," not knowing if he had killed her.

Light and shade, though steadily darkening, intermingle. Crystal and Pedro, in their individual ways, seem at this stage to operate by an emotional charge entirely different from Fox's, simpler, uncalculating, in enthusiasm or dejection, seeing their circumstances, pragmatically, as open to answers. They have none of Fox's vague intuitions of quite another condition of being. With Gabriel there appears a closer identity of feeling, understanding and hostility combined—"we could never get on," Gabriel says; "we're too alike." It is a most impressively written scene, suggesting attitudes reaching up from beneath what is actually spoken.

Gabriel tells Fox of his drifter's life in England and the psychiatrist who "got everything wrong: he worked it out that you were some sort of softy and that Crystal was as tough as nails." He accepts phlegmatically his eventual arrest, hardly speaking—"autistic," as he reported the psychiatrist's diagnosis. Yet it is to Gabriel that Fox confides his fleeting illumination:

> Sick of it all. Not sick so much as desperate; desperate for something that has nothing to do with all this. Restless, Gabby boy, restless. And a man with a restlessness is a savage bugger. . . . I want a dream I think I've had to come true. I want to live like a child. I want to die and wake up in heaven with Crystal.

The past too adds its distinct tone to the chiaroscuro.

Fox supplements Pedro's recollections with his own memory of meeting Crystal, in "the third and last golden van . . . a princess . . . her hair tied up with a royal-blue ribbon, and a blue blouse, and a navy skirt—." These were the halcyon days, "you and me and the old accordion and the old rickety wheel," when on an early morning they "slipped out and raced across the wet fields in our bare feet," unencumbered by possessions and plans of action. It is not exactly this itself, but something it represents, that Fox longs to re-create. It has receded further and further from him in a present that he itches—"a savage bugger"—to destroy. Gabriel, echoing El Cid, is the first to recognize that Fox himself, to get rid of Pedro, poisoned Pedro's dog:

GABRIEL: You're full of hate—that's what's wrong with you—you hate everybody!
FOX: No.
GABRIEL: Even Crystal.
FOX: What about Crystal?
GABRIEL: She'll be the next. You'll ditch her too.

Fox denies it. "My Crystal is the only good part of me." The final scenes strip Fox's protestation, and their entire relationship, to the core. Crystal's father is in hospital, dying, Gabriel under arrest. Van and truck have been sold, the company disbanded. Crystal and Fox are back to their beginnings, but, with all that has passed since then between them, Crystal is drained and sombre in the penultimate scene. The last Episode begins—they are both slightly elated from wine—exu-

berantly, the past regained. All the time, Crystal has
seen through Fox, even his poisoning Gringo, fearful
only of his intentions to her. For Crystal, love is all:
"I really didn't give a damn about any of them, God
forgive me, not even Pedro, not so long as you didn't
turn on me. That's all I cared about."

So she fancies. Fox cannot let it rest. He tells her,
falsely, that he informed on Gabriel for a reward.
Crystal too now leaves him: "I don't know you. . . .
Don't know you at all. . . . Never knew. . . ." Her
knowledge of Fox, though fuller than it seemed, is
like everyone else's, partial, at best of actions, not
motives. He destroys, neither through hatred nor love,
but because of a bewildered groping to understand
them, and what may become of them, what the one
will cause, the other tolerate, what happens to youth
when its hopes have gone and "love alone isn't enough
now . . . not nearly enough." His final speech, as he
spins his wheel, beautifully revolves his inklings of a
truth, some enduring innocence, which in the end he
has not isolated:

> I love you, my Crystal, and you are the best part of
> me, and I don't know where I'm going or what will
> become of me, I might have stumbled on as I did once,
> but I got an inkling, my Crystal, and I had to hold on
> to that . . . red-yellow-black or blue, you pays your
> money and you takes your choice, not that it makes a
> damn bit of difference because the whole thing's fixed,
> my love, fixed-fixed-fixed; [*almost gently*] but who am I
> to cloud your bright eyes or kill your belief that love
> is all. A penny a time and you think you'll be happy
> for life.

As with *The Doctor's Story,* when Pedro dismally
fails as stand-in for El Cid, there is to be no happy
ending for "the hoors." Remorselessly, Fox has stripped
himself of the little he has, to become "naked, un-
accommodated man." He abandons, or offers the as-
sumption that he has abandoned, the only integrity he
ever lays claim to: "I'm not much, sonny," he had told
Gabriel, "but I'm no informer"; and vilifying himself,
he is believed and rejected. "Love is not love," in the
romantic convention, "that alters when it alteration
finds." Here, that is the only love there is. Fox's quest
is not just a death wish. It has a desperate hope in
view, but it leaves him, loving still, denied recourse
to the human ruses for dissembling reality.

All this takes place in a world removed from that
of the earlier plays. In *Philadelphia,* in *Cass,* in *Lovers,*
high spirits, laughter, whatever opposites they may
have to contend with, are genuinely a release. *Crystal
and Fox* has no uncompromised gaiety. At his most
lighthearted, there are reservations in Fox, undeclared
but evident in how he goes about what he says and
does. There are cracks in Fox's behaviour—his bitterness, his enthusiasms and sudden bland indifferences—
which are tokens of the faults beneath. A stage-direc-
tion suggests their nature: *"his exultation . . . has also
a cold brittle quality, and edge of menace."*

In *Crystal and Fox* the menace is always at hand.
Its most obvious manifestation is in physical brutality,
on and off stage, from the motorcycle policeman's silent,
intimidating presence to Gabriel's assault on the old

woman, then his arrest by the two detectives, who rough
him up and threaten worse to come. Fox too, who
poisons Gringo, has a part in this. He does violence
not so importantly to the dog as to Pedro's loyalty and
trust. This violence echoes the destructive impulses in
him that he half willingly lets take command.

In his own small community, Fox sees through the
simple-hearted panaceas for human discontents. In the
world at large, of which Fox's world might be a mi-
crocosm, universal brotherhood and selfless love have
recalcitrant agents to employ. Fox is an itinerant showman who proves what he would rather not believe;
he is also the old Adam part of Everyman.

Human beings do not exist in the steady state of
equations like "I love you," "I hate you," "I despise
you." These formulae homogenize the swerves and
turns that each of *Crystal's* predecessors reveals for its
particular group. Their association with *Crystal* does
not need elaborating. At this point, the differences are
of greater interest.

The setting, and the characters that go with it, are
different in kind. The only—distant—relative of devices
like the Private Gar, direct address to the audience,
the "rhapsodies," is the play-within-the-play and the
audience at Fox's show. There is no Gar to voice hidden thoughts, no Cass to soliloquize. The method of
Crystal is more fully naturalistic. Linguistically, too, it
is in comparison stripped and severe, working to other
purposes the manner of scenes like Master Boyle's leave-
taking in *Philadelphia,* where words touch obliquely
on feelings. These purposes, most important of all,

darken the humor, and in *The Gentle Island,* Friel's
next play, trace in human illusions and suspicion the
roots of violence.

The Gentle Island is Inishkeen, off the Donegal
coast. Most of the islanders, as the play opens, are
leaving: for Glasgow, London, Manchester, where according to Manus Sweeney they will be "Irish Paddys
slaving their guts out in a tunnel all day." Manus
stays on Inishkeen with his two sons, Joe and Philly,
and Philly's wife, Sarah. Two Dublin holiday-makers
join them, the middle-aged Peter Quinn and his pro-
tégé, Shane Harrison. The set is Manus's cottage, with
all its flotsam gathered in the war years, and the street
outside.

Several paths extend from the past, approach each
other, mingle. The communal withdrawal aggravates
existing strains among the Sweeneys. Sarah recalls a
summer as chambermaid on the Isle of Man, when she
wore out three pairs of shoes dancing; and, childless,
broods on Philly, who is "no good to me," going his
self-sufficient way about his chores. Manus dreams of
Joe's bringing back for marriage one of the departed
girls. Oblivious of these tensions, Peter and Shane
precipitate the catastrophe. Their own relationship is
at a crisis. After ten years of "gratitude," Shane increasingly resents the love extorted by Peter: "only
tuppence a week—for a million years."

The island is a major focus of these relationships.
The play asks, but does not explicitly say, what its
nature really is. For Peter it is an Arcadia—"the sea,
the land, fishing, turf-cutting, milking, a house built

by your own great-grandfather, two strong sons to succeed you—everything's so damned constant. You're part of a permanence." Shane is more captious, mocking Manus's legends, and tales of booty taken from the sea: "The place and his way of life and everything he believes in and all he touches—dead, finished, spent. And when he finally faces that, he's liable to become dangerous. . . . Where was I this summer? As a matter of fact I spent four days in a war museum."

Several versions of pastoral discreetly offer comparison. When Shane enters he fools about as a cowboy—"Apache name. Means scalping Island." Struck by the silence, he thinks of the Pied Piper. "Chap in strange uniform up front playing recorder. Young people all laughing and singing. They reach the mountain. A door opens. They all march through. Disappear. Door shuts. Then silence." Later, for Sarah's amusement, he acts the happy "plantation darky." Sarah's commercialized Isle of Man, another Hesperides, is a comment too.

The island in its idyllic summer weather has its beauty, but despite Peter's enchantment it is deceptive. Even when a functioning community, the island was vengeful. Manus's legend of the three rocks is of thwarted love. In another story, a dishonest packman was dragged for a day round the island harnessed behind a maltreated donkey. The islanders' farewell party plays cruel sport with two cats. A dog left behind—"Put a shot in him, will you, Joe"—Manus mutilates with a hay-fork. Horseplay can turn vicious, as Philly's does with Shane. The episodes of violence are the anti-

masque, compromising any sentiment of vernal innocence. They menace the candor and serenity fabricated
by Peter, who does not see how dangerously Philly has
used his spade as they cut turf together. And in the
end, the gun meant for the dog shatters Shane's spine.

Sarah has turned to him for satisfaction—"I want to
lie with you, engineer." He refuses. That evening, she
reports to Manus, she has seen Shane and Philly in the
island boathouse, where "he's doing for the queer what
he couldn't do for me." She calls on Manus for ven-
geance, but after the accusation of Shane, passion
flickering between the brief exchanges, it is Sarah who
fires the gun. Shane may live; he will never walk. In
the coda, Joe quits the island. Manus, Philly, and Sarah
resume a desolate life.

This is in a way Friel's most Irish play. Its point of
departure is the peculiarly regional one of the depopu-
lated offshore islands. The point of departure, however, is exactly that, a certain state of affairs in a particular locality, circumstance, family. Its purpose is not
to elegize the past, to interpret social causes, to at-
tribute any superior "reality" to the simple life. Though
all these notions glance through the action, they are
not its subject, nor does the play tidy them into answers. The action itself generates its own questions.

Shane says flippantly, "And that's the truth, so help
me God. If one admits that there is an ultimate reality,
would the panel agree. . . ." Events, character, and
motives in the play call up like reflections. "They all
like you," Peter assures Shane. "Which of me?" he
replies. What is the truth about Manus's treatment of

his wife, Sarah's version or his own? What happened between Shane and Philly? After telling her story, Sarah simply allows the plausibility of the misunderstandings pleaded by Joe. Whatever the "truth," Manus never abandons the alternatives—"Maybe they only went into the boathouse to change their clothes because they were wet." Conversation slides into words that avoid what the partners to it really have in mind:

> SARAH: You're back.
> PHILLY: Aye.
> SARAH: Tired?
> PHILLY: A bit.
> SARAH: D'you want something to eat?
> PHILLY: I'll have a sleep first.
>   PAUSE. . . .
> SARAH: Maybe if you spent less time on fishing we might be better off.
> PHILLY: Farming? Here?
> SARAH: You and me.
>   PAUSE.
> PHILLY: I'm tired.
> SARAH: You're always tired when you're at home.
> PHILLY: I was up all night, woman. When you and the rest of them were away drinking and dancing I was working.
> SARAH: So you were.
>   *He looks at her uncertain what she means. He opens his mouth to say something more, decides against it, goes into the bedroom.*

The dialogue suggests the conversational assumptions familiar to people who know each other well. There are longer speeches, speakers more elaborately combined, but it is mainly through such taciturnity that the play conveys the pressure and response of human associations, forever renegotiating their terms. Both language and situation are Irish in idiom, but with the celebrated national eloquence—which the play does not repudiate—and gaiety much marked down. Behind other masks the relationships work to their savage outcome.

The whole set of relationships is the matter of the play. It is an unstable grouping of individuals, further jeopardized by Peter and Shane. Joe and Manus take to them amiably, Philly with sardonic calculation. But they are foreign curiosities, half the time, as Sarah says, meaning no more than the voices she picks up on the radio. "Are yous Yanks?" she asks. In a play that does not isolate a principal, she is the commanding figure, a beautifully realized and original creation. Sullen, shrewish, avid, she is also, as in the superb scene where she makes her advances to Shane, vulnerable. She, not Shane, is the tragic waste.

The Gentle Island is not only about Inishkeen. Ireland has been historically, and is, a violent land. The play makes an image of this which, in one aspect, has the significance of Seamus Heaney's "The Last Mummer." It expresses also a sense—or the loss of a sense—of possessing, and of belonging (to farm, region, culture), the ownership of land: closely woven, in Irish life and writing, with the violence and bitterness that Yeats, if he did not commend, acknowledged. More broadly, it is a parable of human groping after communion and permanence, and the elisions of contact that frustrate it. *The Gentle Island* marks a new direction in Friel. It very firmly develops new themes and, in the ways indicated, new methods.

The Gentle Island is as different from its predecessors as *Philadelphia* was, promising a continuing evolution in Friel's approach to his medium and what he has to say in it. The two years after *The Gentle Island* precipitated for him a dramatic fable that insisted upon yet different forms to image the continued Northern violence. *The Freedom of the City*, his most recent play, took shape over those years, though its origins shelve further back. As a play about the present North, set in Derry in 1970, it engages the problem of maintaining the prismatic individuality of character in a situation—that is, the real-life situation—readier to assume the simplicities of political dogma.

Michael, Lily, and Skinner are dead to begin with, identified, as soldiers drag their bodies from the stage, to the Judge conducting the enquiry into their deaths. The stage is fluid. Judge and witnesses make episodic appearances on the wall battlements above the main scene. The Tribunal is literally a framework for the main action. This covers the day when, as rumor and official account agreed, a gang of armed subversives occupied Derry Guildhall, headquarters of the City administration, after the army had broken up a Civil Rights demonstration. Hence a basic irony: events as they were; events as the enquiry elicits and pronounces on them. But we are to be wary, as in *Lovers*, of taking such an irony as anything like the whole story.

Blinded by CS gas, Michael, Lily, and Skinner

stumble into the Mayor's Parlour of the Guildhall. Michael and Lily have been on the march. Skinner is a less certain quantity: a drop-out, irresponsible, cynical. It is he who realizes where they are, at the centre of the building that for Republicans symbolized the Unionist ascendancy. At once he makes free of what it has to offer—drink, telephone, ponderous civic trappings to be contemptuously abused. Lily, at first alarmed by the disrespect, soon joins in. Michael, strong for disciplined protest, remains disapprovingly aloof. So, as they talk of political marches, of Derry, of their lives, a tracery of experience emerges, with the feelings and attitudes grown from it. Outside, the army marshals; people feed on word of insurrection and atrocity; television interprets, a ballad singer mythologizes, the events. All the external accounts are entirely at odds with what we see happen in the Mayor's Parlour.

Finally emerging from the Guildhall, unarmed, Michael, Lily, and Skinner are shot down. Their funerals, heavily graced by dignitaries from the Republic, almost immediately institutionalize their deaths as National Monuments. For the TV commentator, they are notably "dignified," a mirror image of the Civil Rights marches derided by Skinner. The Tribunal has deliberated conflicting eyewitness testimony, and expert evidence, much of it gruesomely clinical. The Judge, on legally sufficient evidence—all he has—finds that the three carried arms and used them; he exonerates the army. The victims, as in their funerals, have become objects, the individuality we have seen of no account.

Michael appears a little pompous, his eyes on the

middle class, half out of the slums, full of Civil Rights doctrine. He regrets the vanished "dignity" of the earliest marches, when the presence of "doctors, teachers, accountants," impressed him. "Shite," says Skinner, impatient of respectability. Michael is in part what Skinner mocks, an easy butt. Yet he has an appealingly bewildered honesty, touchingly uncertain. The circumstances that supplied his answers, he uneasily suspects, have gone.

Lily, ignorant and artless, forty-three years old, with eleven children, is most fully of her background, spokeswoman for ghetto miseries she hardly sees as injuries. Her world is the streets around her, their life her conversation, indifferently of suffering, brutality, high spirits:

> below us Celia Cunningham's about half-full now and crying about the sweepstake ticket she bought and lost when she was fifteen. And above us Dickie Devine's groping under the bed for his trombone and he doesn't know yet that Annie pawned it on Wednesday for the wanes bus fares and he's going to beat the tar out of her when she tells him. And down the passage aul Andy Boyle's lying in bed, because he has no coat. And I'm here in the mayor's parlour, dressed up like the duchess of Kent and drinking port wine. I'll tell you something, Skinner: it's a very unfair world.

It is entirely from such facts that Lily articulates her being. The demands of Civil Rights—"wan man, wan vote," "no more gerrymandering"—though she marches for them, are exotic abstractions in her life. So Skinner, over her protests, tells her.

It is the one point in the play where Skinner elaborates any belief. He is clownish, frivolous, caustically dismissive. Approaching statements, he backs away from them: "But we'll discuss it some other time. And as I say, if you're passing this way, don't let them entertain you in the outer office." Lily breaks down the "defensive flippancy" of an acute intelligence that has opted for safety in cultivated indifference.

Lily marches, Skinner says, because she's obscurely aware of outrage at the hardships so vividly expressed in her uncalculating chronicles; because, "in a vague groping way," she has awakened to "hundreds, thousands, millions of us all over the world. . . . It's about us—the poor—the majority—stirring in our sleep. And if that's not what it's all about, then it has nothing to do with us." His statement is liable to be taken as the play's point of view. It is not, like Michael's, undermined by mockery.

Yet how valid does the play make it appear? For Skinner, at that moment, a vision of the unified poor is the only motive with any reality. But those are not Lily's terms, though some response to them may crystallize her own moving formulation:

LILY: Did you ever hear tell of a mongol child, Skinner?
SKINNER: Where did you hide the brandy?
LILY: I told you a lie about our Declan. That's what Declan is. He's not just shy, our Declan. He's a mongol.
          (She finds the brandy bottle and hands it to him.)
          And it's for him I go on all the civil rights marches. . . . Isn't that the stupidest thing you ever heard? Sure I could march and protest from

here to Dublin and sure what good would it do
Declan? But I still march—every Saturday I still
march. Isn't that the stupidest thing you ever
heard?

SKINNER: No.

LILY: That's what the chairman said when I—you
know—when I tried to tell him what I was thinking. He never talks about him; can't even look
at him. And that day that's what he said, "You're
a bone stupid bitch. No wonder the kid's bone
stupid too." The chairman—that's what he said.

Each of the protagonists has a version of reality. In
common their versions share pity, and a potential
anger, for the condition of the poor. The play's "point
of view" is to particularize that condition in these lives.

They reveal the circumstances of "the sub-culture of
poverty," as it is called by Dodds, an American sociolo-
gist who, in three appearances, detached from the action, generalizes on the subject to the audience. The
events are dramatizing the kinds of fact distanced, for
all its understanding, by his urbane commentary. It
is indeed, as he says and as we see, a culture that is
breaking up. However miserable, ghetto life had for
Lily its reassuring familiarities. Ambitions such as
Michael's, ideas like Skinner's, threaten its vehemently
local integrity and domestic loyalties. Would they sur-
vive Skinner's internationalism; and by what, without
them, would that be supported? The world in which
Lily suffered sustained her too, and is collapsing into
problematical shapes.

For the earnest enquirer after historical precision,
"Derry 1970" raises problems. At that time, for ex-

ample, Civil Rights marches, and the early demands they pressed, had stopped; the army was not involved in quite the kind of situation presented in the play; it gives no place to the I.R.A., as a real force, nor to the other imitative private armies. The play is historically selective, conflating features of the pre- and post-internment periods. It thus represents the beginnings of the turmoil. It also intimates their development: civilian/army clashes; and in Skinner, for instance, an intelligence that might follow its logic to the politically more sophisticated endorsements of violence.

This is not to say that *The Freedom of the City* states, or purports to state, all the multiplying symptoms of the distemper—such as the mindlessness of random sectarian killings—except in the general sense that it depicts violence, which, like Shakespeare's "appetite," is "an universal wolf." Nor does it address Protestant motives and compulsions. In its social or political register, the play is drawing only on certain "components of a scene." It is new, for Friel, in taking up directly political occasions. But the difference is a superficial one. It is as ever in individual lives that Friel finds his scene most eloquently present.

Through these lives Friel observes an urban face— and catches the urban as accurately as the rural voice —of the society familiar in his work. He has observed in it its "peculiar spiritual, and indeed material, flux." The imprint of that we may identify, for example, in Gar or in Fox; as we may, differently manifested, in *The Freedom of the City*, the same individual search

4

Conclusion

Drama in the last decade or so has not wanted for industrious, indeed frantic, experiment. Audiences have seen, among other enterprises, Happenings, Black Comedy, Multi-Media Theater and the Theaters of Cruelty, Fact, and the Absurd. Ireland too has had its dramatic upsurge, less extravagant in its forms and, no doubt, if one excepts Beckett, less international in its impact. Besides Friel, the recent dramatists writing in English include Tom Murphy, John B. Keane, Hugh Leonard, Eugene McCabe, Tom Kilroy, Wesley Burrowes, and James Douglas.

There is no point in attempting capsule judgments of these writers, still less in ordering them into some kind of competitive league, or defining them by categories of subject or convention. They have all produced work, of varying power, that continues a capacious Irish dramatic tradition going back to Shaw, and the generations of playwrights mainly associated with the Abbey. Certainly, a play like Kilroy's *The Death and Resurrection of Mr. Roche* is in part brought into being by the generally greater tolerance, not notably an Irish quality, about subject matter, especially concerning sex. Pressures that were largely external have ended the days when Alan Simpson's production of *The Rose Tattoo* was prosecuted in Dublin for obscenity.

To their credit, most Irish writers have consistently kept up their resistance to all the direct and indirect constraints on expression. They were consequently able to benefit from the broad indulgence of unorthodox ideas, and at the same time to retain their hold on Irish themes and their own modes of thought and expression. *Mr Roche* is a beneficiary of liberalization; it is still essentially an Irish play.

The Irish dramatic movement over the past ten years is still generally identifiable with the lines represented by Synge and O'Casey. Peasants and proletariat are commonly the subjects, though boarding houses, furnished apartments, even middle-class drawing-rooms, have occupied part of the scene. The peasants and proletariat, too, are different from their forebears, and the difference is a large part of the topic.

Naturally, the Irish theater is not exclusively home reared. Its writers know and are responsive to Beckett, Osborne, Wesker, Pinter, Albee, and the rest, whose work is a contemporary restatement of the claims of dramatic form. Hugh Leonard writing about Dublin sophisticates, or would-be sophisticates, Tom Kilroy about lonely clerks in dingy flats, are trying to assimilate what they find relevant in the statement to their own themes. That is how the influence works, and is of course how it should work, not toward the modeling of plastic Pinters.

Of these Irish dramatists, Friel has unquestionably the body of work most distinguished by its substance, integrity, and development, well able to stand with that of his English contemporaries. Their writing has a variety and intensity which, even where he does not particularly take to it, Friel much admires. There is no question, however, of an "influence" from any of these sources other than in the indirect way described. Nor is it easy to enter Friel into any of the Irish "schools." His plays are obviously not isolated from the Irish traditions; but he is a Northern Catholic, the first important dramatist from that background, which inflects his distinctive, personal voice.

"I would like," he has said, "to write a play that would capture the peculiar spiritual, and indeed material, flux, that this country is in at the moment. This has got to be done, for me anyway, at a local, parochial level, and hopefully this will have meaning for other people in other countries." This is a fair description of the plays Friel has already written, regarded as a composite, a single, continuing testimony. Their content has its own interest, but the content does not explain their force. Henry James asserted the supremacy of "the compositional contribution," which confers imaginative truth upon the unworked material. In each of his plays Friel achieves the process of dramatic organization, the conjunction of its parts, that discovers order in observed facts, and conveys their meaning. In each of them too, in R. L. Stevenson's phrase, he has varied his method and changed the point of attack.

This inventive command of design gives Friel's plays

their excellence. He has remarked that when Shakespeare wanted to make a point he stated it bluntly, usually three times; in other words, he is sensible of the particular demands imposed by the passing traffic of the stage. Nevertheless, a play does not make its effects only on the large canvas. The totality of experience in the theater consists of accumulating particulars. Fox's final speech, for example, and a couple that precede it, broadly approximate a "meaning" of the play's fable. But it is qualified and augmented by the images—in actions and words—of fulfillment, decay, envy, trust, which less bluntly insist on a hearing from the audience.

What matters, however, is the ultimate end of such means, the convincing familiarity of character and event, bringing to mind the ways of life itself, just as dramatic speech, while it orchestrates, must hold the tune of the spoken word. The audience is to instruct itself from, to quote Friel again, "a set of people and a situation presented with a certain clarity and understanding and sympathy." Both his short stories and his plays supply the creative premises where writer and audience collaborate. In the plays his development has been toward a greater simplicity, but no less subtlety, of method. Friel will continue to find the dramatic forms that generalize, with humor and compassion, on his particular and regional veracities, where art begins.

Selective Bibliography

A. WORKS

(Note: This bibliography does not include occasional writings, e.g., radio talks, or plays and stories written for radio.)

1. Short stories: *The Saucer of Larks.* London: Gollancz, 1962.

   The Gold in the Sea. London: Gollancz, 1966.

2. Plays: *Philadelphia, Here I Come!* London: Faber & Faber, 1965.

   The Loves of Cass McGuire. London: Faber & Faber, 1967.

   Lovers. London: Faber & Faber, 1969.

   Crystal and Fox. London: Faber & Faber, 1970.

   (with *The Mundy Scheme.* New York: Farrar, Straus & Giroux, 1970.

   The Gentle Island (MS, 1971).

   The Freedom of the City (MS, 1972).

B. SELECTED REVIEWS

1. Short Stories: *The Saucer of Larks. New York*

111

Times, June 30, 1962, p. 17; *Atlantic Monthly* 210 (Sept. 1962) :
124; *New Statesman* (March 8,
1963) , p. 349; *Times Literary Supplement* (April 19, 1963) , p. 261.
*The Gold in the Sea. Times Literary
Supplement* (April 28, 1966) , p.
361; *New York Times Book Review* 71 (Oct. 16, 1966) , p. 64;
Critic 25 (Oct./Nov. 1966) : 116;
Hudson Review 19 (Winter 1966/
67) : 673.

2. Plays: *Philadelphia, Here I Come! Guardian* (Oct.
8, 1964) , p. 9; *Drama* (Winter 1965) , p. 51;
Time (Feb. 25, 1966), p. 100; *The New
Yorker* 42 (Feb. 26, 1966) : 71; *Saturday
Review* 49, March 5, 1966.
The Loves of Cass McGuire. Time 88 (Oct.
14, 1966) : 93; *The New Yorker* 42 (Oct. 15,
1966) : 118; *Saturday Review* 49 (Oct. 22,
1966) : 73; *Drama* (Spring 1968) , p. 56.
Lovers. Times (April 20, 1968), p. 21; *Time*
(Aug. 2, 1968) , p. 49; *The New Yorker*
44 (Aug. 3, 1968) : 65; *Drama* (Winter 1969),
pp. 18–19.